GAUGUIN

PAINTINGS

Introduction by
Michelangelo Masciotta

Geddes & Grosset

Translated by Christopher Clark
Edited and adapted by Colin Clark

First published 1978

First published in this edition 1990
Published by Geddes & Grosset Ltd, David Dale House, New Lanark, Scotland

ISBN 1 85534 008 9

Printed in Yugoslavia

CONTENTS

Gauguin

Before he ever used a brush and canvas professionally, Gauguin was a collector of paintings. We know that while working for the stock-exchange firm of Bertin in the 1870s he bought the works of Impressionist artists like Manet, Cézanne, Renoir, Sisley, Pissarro, Monet, and Guillaumin, artists who were to be his colleagues at the fifth Impressionist exhibition in 1880, and that he used his analysis of their techniques and approach as a launching pad for his own new style. Above all, Gauguin looked to the works of Cézanne, which he copied and re-expressed in his own last still lifes, even if his style is less turgid. But more than a lesson in painting, Impressionism represented for Gauguin a recognition of culture. It was a means of seeing the world differently from the way it had been seen before, demonstrating a desire to live in a more natural world, open to the light and the possibilities of the present as well as the hopes of the future. Gauguin even used the technique of juxtaposition — a primary colour next to a supplementary one, a red next to a green, a yellow next to a violet — but with a freedom and casualness that Monet would never have accepted.

We must consider the few lines that Gauguin wrote from Copenhagen on January 14, 1885, to his friend Schuffenecker in Paris: 'The straight line gives the infinite, the curve limits creation. . . . Noble tones exist, common tones exist, harmonies that are peaceful and consoling; and there are others that excite you with their ardour. . . . The equilateral triangle is the most solid and most perfect form for a triangle. A subtle triangle is more elegant. In pure truth there are no sides: for our sensibility, lines exist, those on the right proceed, those on the left recede.' We could almost be reading before their time the words of the Russian-born painter Wassily Kandinsky, one of the first painters of abstract art and author of the now famous *Art of Spiritual Harmony,* first published in 1912. But Gauguin wrote these words in 1885, the same year in which Vincent Van Gogh painted what is probably the most gloomy painting of the nineteenth century, *The potato eaters,* and the naturalistic novelist and art critic, Joris Karl Huysmans published his novel *A Rebours,* which describes a sensualist seeking new experience by deliberately and perversely abusing the senses — art for the sake of art. Gauguin belongs to neither one side nor the other. He is unique, with a character that begins to reveal itself as the sum of his agonies and his ecstasies.

After a period in Copenhagen, Gauguin moved to Brittany, not only because life was cheaper there than in Paris, but much more because the countryside and the people were more straightforward. His painting became more relaxed, more affable. The colours were spread in precise patches, each patch marked by a black line, and the composition is developed in warm tints almost entirely in the foreground, advancing towards the viewer. Bushes, trees, rocks, women in costume alternate in a constant stream of images and imagination. It is almost possible in these paintings to see clearly that which cannot normally be seen, the 'soul', the element which is above or beyond and which we can only glimpse. We can already sense the adoption of a new style which is no longer a matter of lines and points nor coloured areas but is a fact of life, a spiritual conquest. This is particularly true of *The yellow Christ* (Buffalo, New York), one of the most disturbing works in modern painting, which was completed during Gauguin's second stay in Brittany, in 1889. In this *Christ* we see at the same time both the present and a regret for the past, that mixture of simplicity and convention found in works from the late Romanesque and early Gothic periods. Against the short arms of the Cross, as massive as the walls of a country church, the suffering figure of Christ is in contrast to the three grieving women. Christ is in harmony with the new village among the green meadows, with the red of the trees, and is revealed in a totally original light. The forms of the painting are based on the relationship between straight lines, curved lines and colour. The warm colours, yellow and red, are in the centre and the cold colours are above and below, contrary to artistic tradition but giving these few square metres of painted canvas a dimension and value which are immeasurable.

Gauguin gives us further proof of the complexity of his work in Brittany in another painting from the same period, the portrait of Angela Satre, *La belle Angèle* (Paris) which was refused by the sitter, perhaps because she found herself to be 'too much of a peasant' in it. The portrait was really understood, however, by Van Gogh who wrote to his brother, 'The woman looks a bit like a young cow, but there is something so fresh and peasant-like about her that it is a joy to see'.

In 1891 Gauguin left France for Tahiti. His first visit lasted two years, and he returned to Paris in 1893, but in 1895 he was back in Tahiti again. By then he had made up his mind to live far from the clamour of the world and all the dangers of bourgeois society. There, in the distant lands of Oceania, he was able to express himself freely, to give vent to all his desires.

In Tahiti, in 1891, he had already painted the *'Ia Orana Maria' (Hail Mary)* (New York, Metropolitan Museum), a vital painting in Gauguin's story, religious in both a particular and in a general sense. To the painter, religion appeared as being outwith all normal pre-established rules, as an indistinct, superhuman aspiration, a reality immersed in a time without history, but alive everywhere, in every country. It assumed the characteristics and revealed the hopes and desires of peoples of every country. It was a myth which was continually being renewed, into a pantheism that followed the laws of nature, as still as the trees, as fluid as the waters of a river, changing colour from hour to hour, and from country to country. In the painting, the angel with the yellow wings who can just be made out on the left, blending in with the leaves and branches, is the small figure of a Maori boy. Mary is dressed in the clothes of the women of Oceania, and the two faithful have naked breasts and the *pareo,* the sarong-type skirt, wrapped around their waists. The little Jesus is naked, fresh, the spirit of life, the contrary of the *tupapau,* the spirit of death. He is the spirit who watches over. A year later, behind the splendid young girl lying flat on the blue and yellow pareo that she uses as a sheet, he becomes the spirit of death, the hour which brings to an end all our actions, *'Manau tupapau' (The spirit of the dead keeps watch)* (Buffalo, New York). This is a natural fact: life connected to death, death to life. This is the way it is, and the primitive accepts this human condition and proclaims the generating principle of our passage through the world, its mystery.

Love of the exotic tends to make us denigrate the acts and customs of Western civilization and to exalt the mysterious revelations of primitive peoples. Gauguin was both fascinated and perturbed by this. But not even the innnocence of these brown people, the brown that he so admired and that he painted with golden reflections, was enough to placate him. Instead, his dismay deepened from year to year. Paris was far away, and he knew he would not return there. He also knew that his life was bound to evil, and that you cannot struggle against your destiny. He carried on dreaming, even though his dreams were made up of nightmares. The idea of death was identified with the idol with raised arms, and the idol called him. It was the overwhelming thought of suicide that led him to compose the work which could be called his saga of Tahiti, the enormous canvas

'D'Où venons-nous? Que sommes-nous? Où allons-nous?' (Where are we from? What are we? Where are we going?) (Boston). Gauguin himself told us how to interpret it, from right to left. We come from an unknown world where the fauna is represented by a black and white dog only half seen. The flora, the trees growing out of the water and the rocks, spread their branches over a sleeping child who is humanity, just entering earthly life. Three seated young women are ready to live their youthful days of pleasure, two standing women dressed in purple represent the mystery which awaits them, and the seated woman, one arm upraised, sits beside them motionless, as if to signify that no change is possible. In spite of this, life should be enjoyed, its sweet and splendid fruits should be plucked, the way the young man on his feet does in the middle of the painting. In this erect figure, Gauguin encapsulates the spirit of the elements, earth, water and sky, that can bring happiness to man. But there

is also a simple life, expressed in the boy sitting down, eating an apple, two cats and a goat by his side. And there is an ambiguous life, composed of vanity, which is embodied in the eye-catching animal that resembles a peacock. But life does not stand still, it flows on, albeit irregularly, until it encounters the mute idol with bluish shadows. Truth is still to be discovered, still to be faced up to, beyond all barriers. A lovely, almost totally naked girl is aware of the call of mystery, an old lady is absorbed in her own thoughts, awaiting the end. The scene is finished off by the strange white bird that has come from who knows where and is heading who knows where, a symbol of the uselessness of things and words.

The eroticism that was one of the most violent aspects of Gauguin, the man and the artist, faded away following his attempted suicide, immediately after finishing *D'Où venons-nous?* The French poet and Symbolist, Stéphane Mallarmé, said of *The White Horse* (Paris, Musée d'Orsay), 'It is amazing that so much mystery can be put in so much light'. In *Two Tahitian women ('Les seins aux fleurs rouges')* (New York, Metropolitan Museum), the light comes closer, entering the bodies and falling on the breasts and on the red mango flowers of the women who seem awed by their own beauty, by the awareness of their new purpose in the world — to live, at last, without sin. This light penetrates the spirit of the painter, with its memories of happier years, with the knowledge of having succumbed to evil forces, with the desire for a beauty that has been glimpsed but never possessed.

In 1902, a year before his death, Gauguin expressed these feelings once again in *'Contes barbares' (Barbarous tales)* (Essen). At one side kneels a friend from his time in Brittany, the dwarf painter Jacob Meyer de Haan. In front of him sits an idol in the form of a woman, composed in a perfect axis, like a Buddha, and, as an essential fulfilment, to the right kneels the woman he has always been seeking and has now found in an enchantingly beautiful form. This particular figure has reminded many, quite understandably, of a Botticelli angel. The model for it was probably Tehotaua, an inhabitant of the island of Hiva Oa in the Marquesas islands, where Gauguin had moved in 1901. In 1902, he wrote to Daniel de Monfried, a fellow-artist and good friend, 'You cannot imagine what a peaceful life I live here', but soon after he was again involved in quarrels and had antagonized many of those around him. He died on May 8, 1903, alone and lonely, but however painful periods of his life may have been, his belief in himself and in his art has long been vindicated by the ineradicability of his mark on twentieth-century painting.

Biographical Details

1848 June 7 — Paul Gauguin is born in Paris to Clovis Gauguin, a liberal journalist, and Aline Marie Chazal, daughter of André Chazal, a printmaker, and Flora Tristan, a writer.

1851 Because of his father's liberal politics, the family goes to live in Lima, Peru, with relatives of his mother. His father dies on the journey.

1855 Paul returns to France and goes through his regular studies at Orleans, living in the house of his paternal uncle, before attending naval college in Paris.

1865 He goes to sea, first in the merchant navy, then in the French navy. He travels round the world, visiting India, Brazil and the South Seas.

1867 His mother dies, naming the stockbroker and art collector, Gustave Arosa, as his guardian.

1871 Paul returns to Paris and through the good offices of Gustave Arosa takes a job in the stock-exchange firm of Bertin.

1873 He marries Mette Sophie Gad, a Danish girl from a comfortably off home. In the next ten years they have five children. He begins attending evening art classes at the Academie Colarossi and spending Sundays painting *en plein air*.

1874 The first Impressionist exhibition is held in Paris. He has met the painter Camille Pissarro, and begins studying with him.

1876 One of his landscape paintings is accepted for exhibition at the Salon.

1877 The family rents a house from a sculptor from whom Gauguin learns the basics of modelling.

1879 By now Gauguin has begun collecting the work of other painters. He takes part in the fourth Impressionist exhibition in April.

1880 He shows seven paintings and a bust of Mette at the fifth Impressionist exhibition. His work is showing its own characteristics and moving away from Impressionism.

1881 He shows at the sixth Impressionist exhibition. Although still working as a stockbroker, he spends the summer painting with Pissarro and Cézanne at Pontoise.

1882 He shows ten paintings and one sculpture at the seventh Impressionist exhibition. There is a crash on the Paris stock exchange.

1883 The stock-market crash of 1882 is affecting the stock market, so Gauguin decides that he can make a living from painting alone. In October he moves his pregnant wife and four children to Rouen.

1884 In the autumn, Mette and three of the children leave Rouen to live in Copenhagen. Gauguin and the other two follow a month later.

1885 Gauguin does not find Denmark sympathetic and in the summer returns to Paris with his son Clovis who is later sent to boarding school. Gauguin also visits Dieppe and London and works for a time as a bill-poster in Paris.

1886 He shows nineteen works at the eighth and last Impressionist exhibition. In June he moves to Brittany to paint at Pont-Aven and in October returns to Paris. He begins his interest in ceramic sculpture.

1887 In April he travels with the painter Charles Laval to Panama where he visits his sister and works as a labourer on the Panama Canal. He is ill with yellow fever and dysentery, but moves on to Martinique where he remains for four months and paints several pictures. On his return to Paris in the autumn he meets the Van Gogh brothers, Vincent and Theo.

1888 In February he returns to Brittany for his second stay at Pont-Aven. Here, he and Emile Bernard create the Synthetist movement, based on the Symbolist movement in literature. It ignores naturalism to allow artists to use simple planes of strong colour and black line to express moods, emotion, and ideas. In October he goes to work with Van Gogh at Arles. But after two months the famous quarrel takes place. Gauguin returns to Paris four months earlier than planned.

1889 In June he returns to Brittany, this time to the isolated village of Le Pouldu. Here he paints, makes wood carvings, designs furniture and ceramic sculpture, and helps decorate Marie Henry's inn in the village. In this year he first writes art criticism and takes up printmaking.

1890 He spends the summer at Le Pouldu and is planning his trip to Tahiti.

1891 He visits Copenhagen to say goodbye to his family. On April 1, he leaves for Tahiti. When he arrives in June, he stays in Papeete, the capital, but, finding it too European, in September moves to a bamboo hut in the village of Mataiea where he begins work in earnest.

1892 He studies all aspects of Polynesian culture, using as his source an account of the ancient beliefs and customs of Tahiti by a Belgian explorer, and writes to his wife that 'I feel I am beginning to understand the Oceanic character'. Mette begins to have a little success selling his paintings. His work is showing the influence of Polynesian mythology which he mixes with themes from European Symbolism. He uses as a model a young Polynesian girl, Teha'amana, with whom he goes through a form of marriage approved by her parents.

1893 Gauguin continues to develop his synthesis of European and Oceanic themes and symbols, but shortage of funds requires him to return to Europe. He leaves Tahiti on June 14 and arrives in Marseilles in August. In Paris, he continues to paint Tahitian subjects, using as a model a girl of Indian and Malay origin, Anna, who calls herself Javanese. He begins to write an account of his time in Tahiti, *Noa Noa,* which is to be illustrated with woodcuts, a medium he masters quickly.

1894 His uncle in Orleans dies and Gauguin inherits a legacy of 13,000 francs. He refuses to share it with Mette, who finally breaks off communication with him. In April, Gauguin returns to Pont-Aven in Brittany with Anna. As well as woodcuts, he has taken up the medium of watercolour monotypes.

1895 By now Gauguin is estranged from many of his friends as well as from his wife. He returns to Tahiti on June 29, leaving the text and woodcuts of *Noa Noa* with the poet Charles Morice for revision. He arrives in Papeete on September 8. He builds a house with a studio at Puinaauia, where Teha'amana, who has given birth to his son and then taken a Tahitian husband, joins him but remains only a week. Another girl, Pau'ura a Tai, comes to live with him, and he uses her as a model.

1896 Because of ill health, Gauguin does little painting. To earn money, he teaches drawing to the daughters of a French landowner, Auguste Goupil, and paints portraits of the family. He continues his lifelong propensity to argue with officialdom and antagonizes the Catholic mission by placing 'pagan' sculptures in his garden.

1897 Again Gauguin is in financial trouble and is ill. He moves house, takes a bank loan and builds another house. His favourite daughter dies. He begins to despair and, at the very end of the year, after completing his enormous philosophical painting, *D'Où venons-nous?*, he decides to commit suicide by poisoning himself with arsenic. The attempt fails.

1898 He receives money from Paris to pay off his debts. He takes a job as a draughtsman. He continues to send paintings back to France for exhibition in the Vollard gallery. He takes up journalism and becomes involved in local politics. Pau'ura gives birth to a son whom Gauguin names Emil, the same as his first child by Mette. This inspires him to paint again.

1901 He reaches a financial arrangement with Vollard for twenty-five paintings a year. This allows him to give up his job, and he decides to leave Tahiti for 'a more primitive place'. On September 16, he arrives at Atuono on the island of Hiva Oa in the Marquesas. His eyesight is beginning to fail, but the move inspires him to renewed vigour, producing oil paintings and monotypes. A local girl, Vaeho, moves in with him.

1902 More and more, Gauguin takes to writing, setting down his philosophy of art and his reminiscences. Again, he antagonizes local colonial officials and churchmen.

1903 On May 8, Gauguin dies. Because of his quarrel with the church he is refused a Christian burial

1906 A major retrospective exhibition of Gauguin's work is held in the Salon d'Autonne in Paris. This has a profound effect on the new generation of artists, such as Matisse, Derain, and Picasso, who will mould the art of the twentieth century.

Geographical Index of Paintings

THE PAINTINGS

The Seine with the bridge of Jena and detail (overleaf), 1875.
Oil on canvas, 65 × 92 cm ($25\frac{5}{8} \times 36\frac{1}{4}$ in).
Paris, Musée d'Orsay.

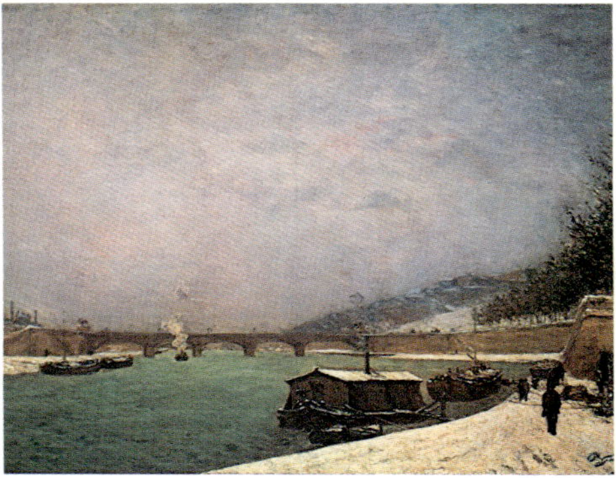

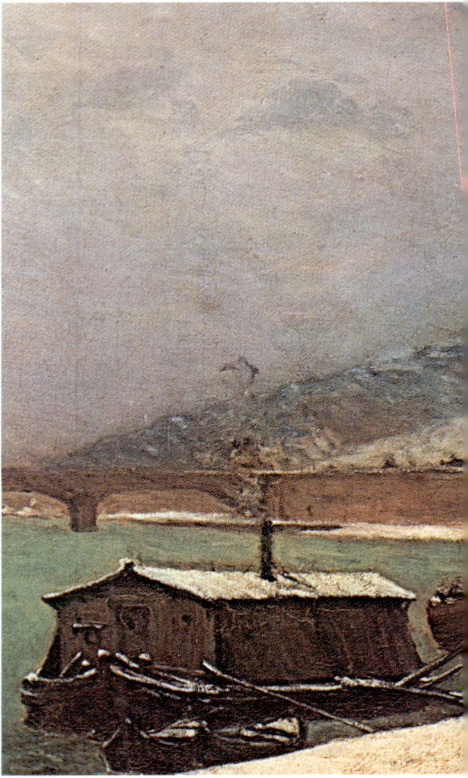

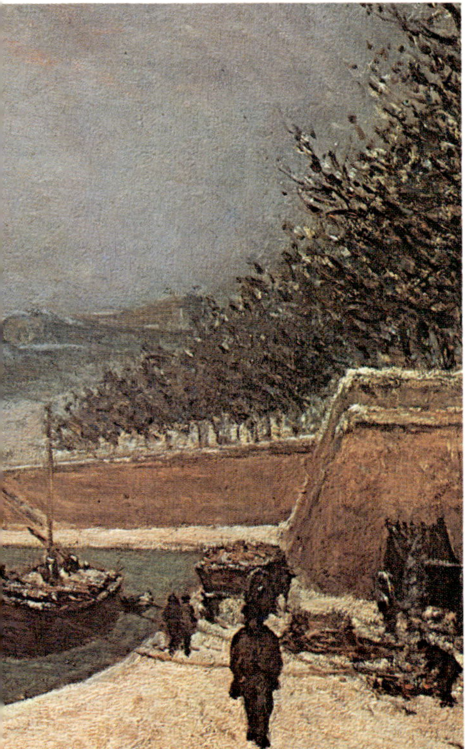

The washerwomen of Pont-Aven and
detail (overleaf), 1886.
Oil on canvas, 71 × 90 cm (28 × 35½ in).
Paris, Musée d'Orsay.

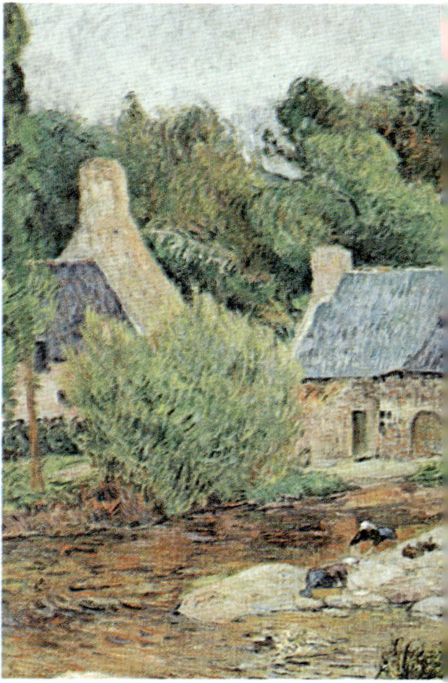

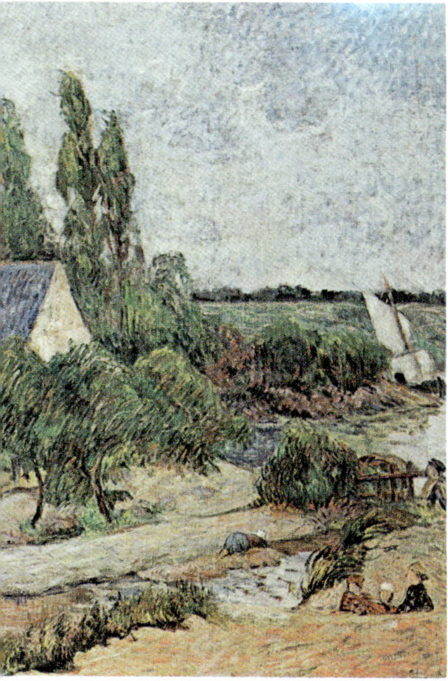

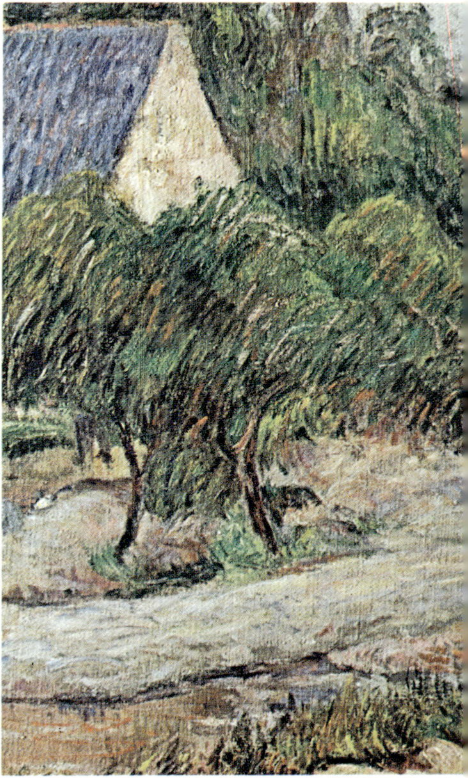

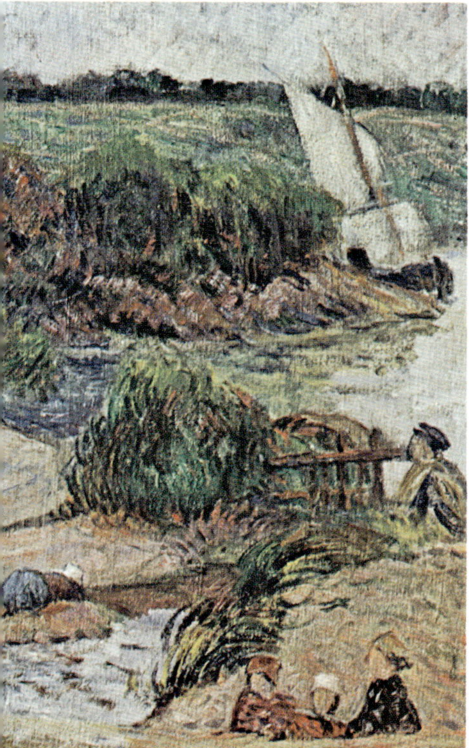

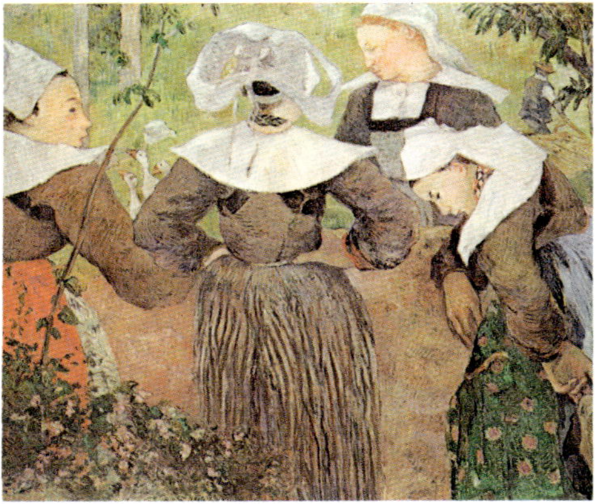

'Les quatres Bretonnes' (The four Breton women) and details (opposite and overleaf), 1886.
Oil on canvas, 72 × 90 cm ($28\frac{3}{8}$ × $35\frac{1}{2}$ in).
Munich, Neue Pinakothek.

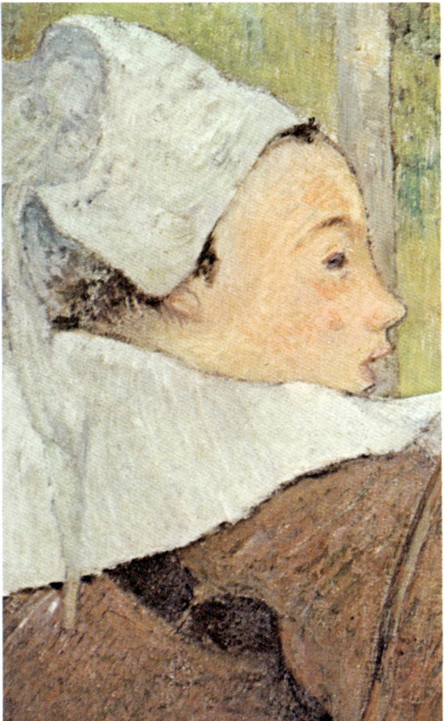

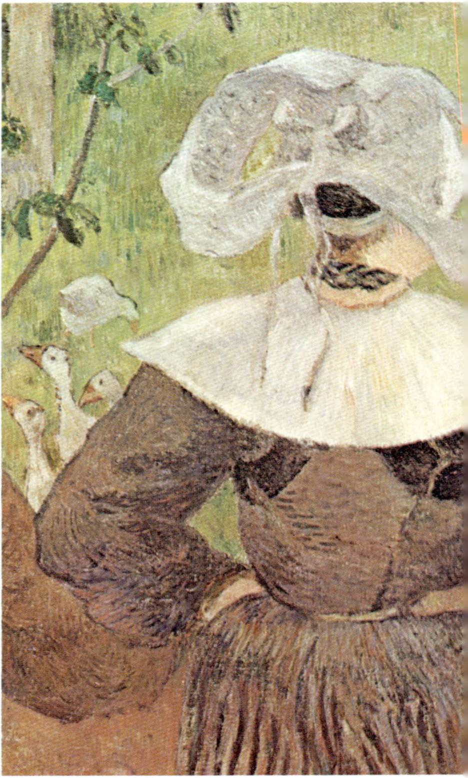

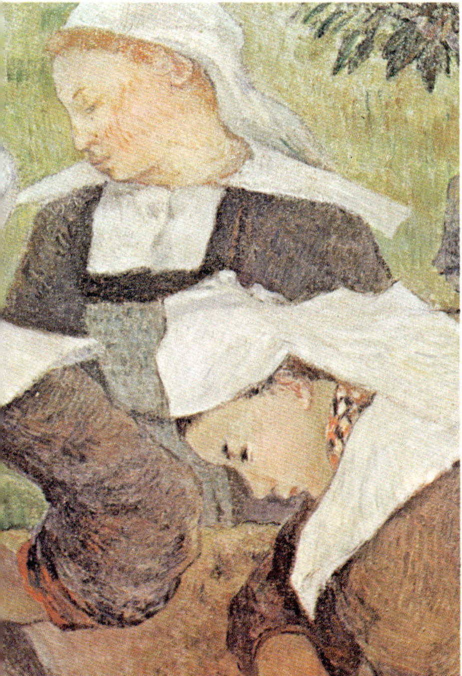

Peasants and a haystack 1889.
Oil on canvas, 72 × 92 cm
(28¾ × 36¼ in).
Paris, Musée d'Orsay.

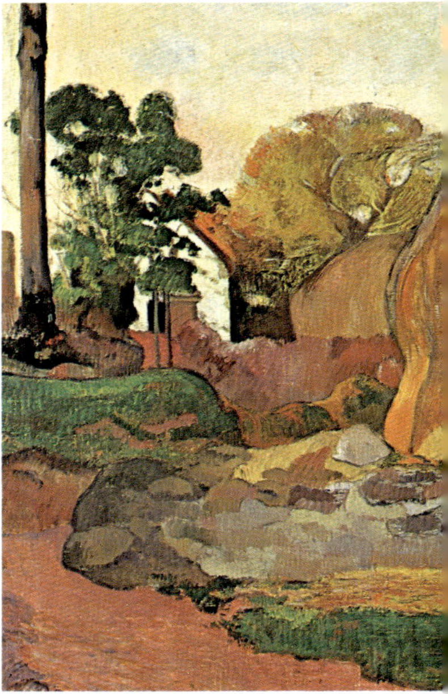

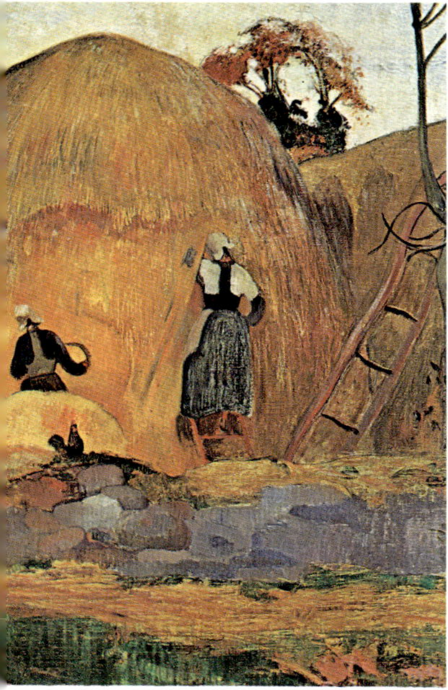

The pool between the trees and detail (opposite), 1887.
Oil on canvas, 90 × 116 cm ($35^{1}/_{2}$ × $45^{5}/_{8}$ in).
Munich, Neue Pinakothek.

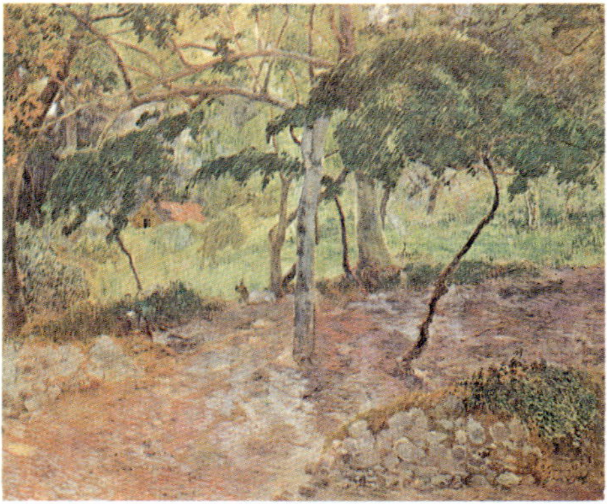

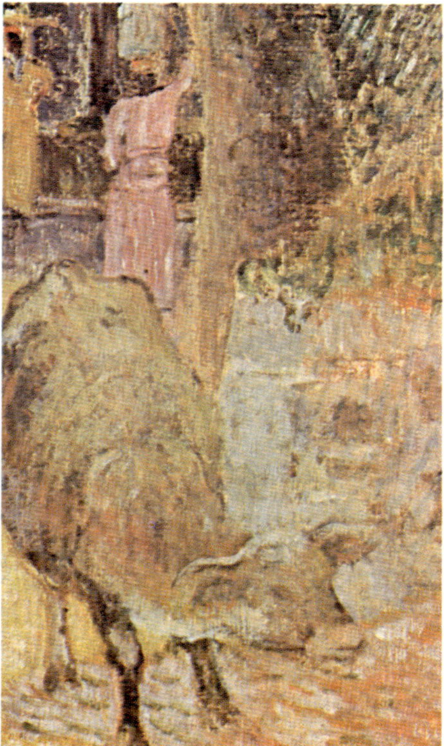

Gathering the hay 1888.
Oil on canvas, 73 × 92 cm ($28^3/_4$ × $36^1/_4$ in).
Paris, Musée d'Orsay.

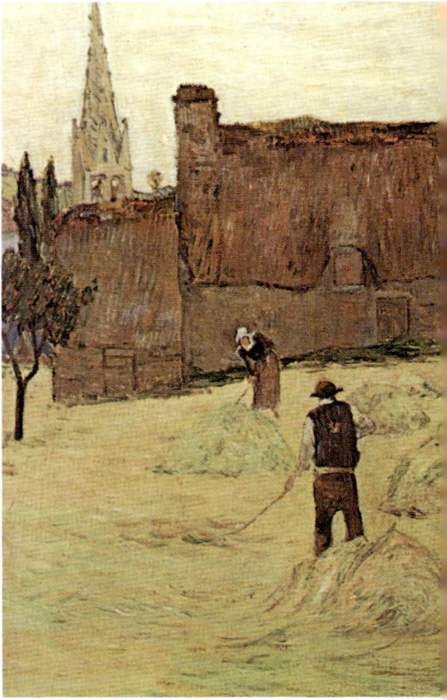

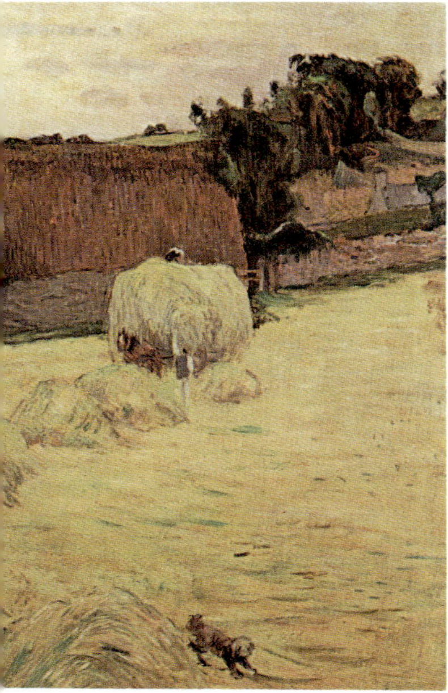

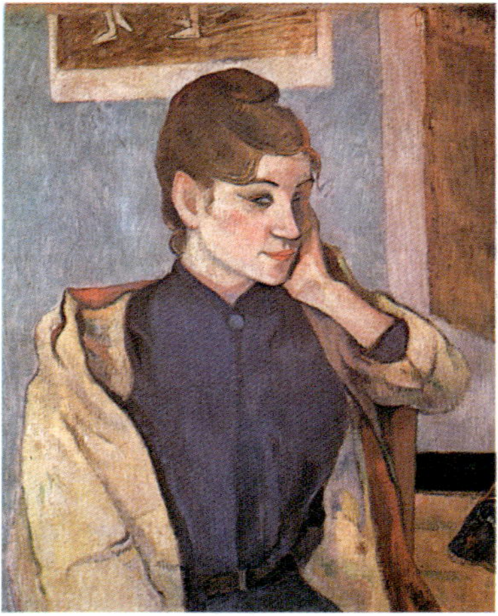

Madeleine Bernard and detail (opposite), 1888.
Oil on canvas, 72 ×58 cm ($28\frac{3}{8} \times 22\frac{7}{8}$ in).
Grenoble, Musée de Peinture et de Sculpture.

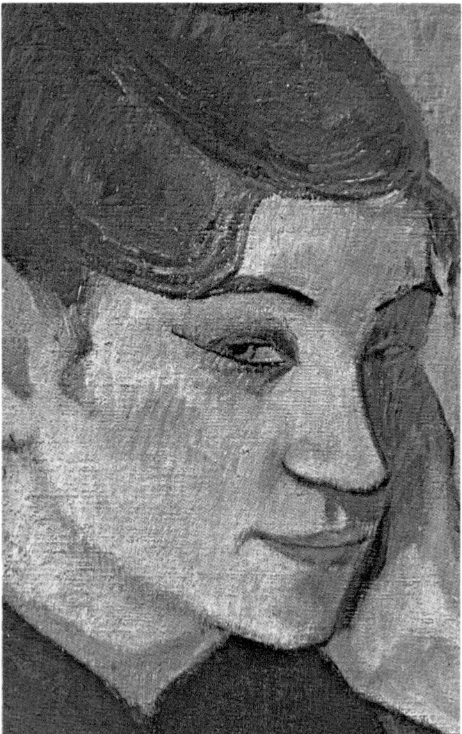

View of the Alyschamps and detail (opposite), 1888.
Oil on canvas, 92 × 73 cm ($36\frac{1}{4}$ × $28\frac{3}{4}$ in).
Paris, Musée d'Orsay.

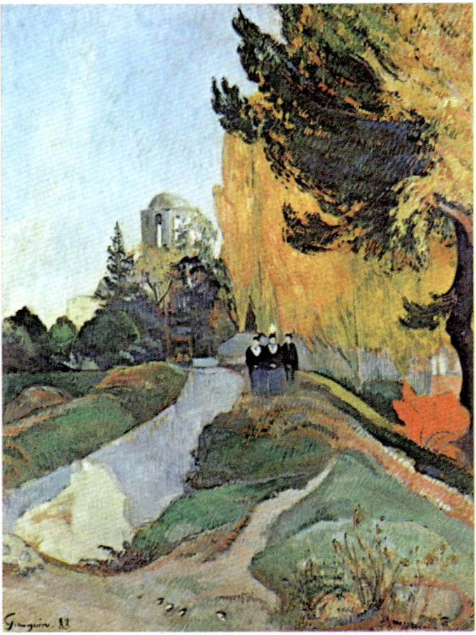

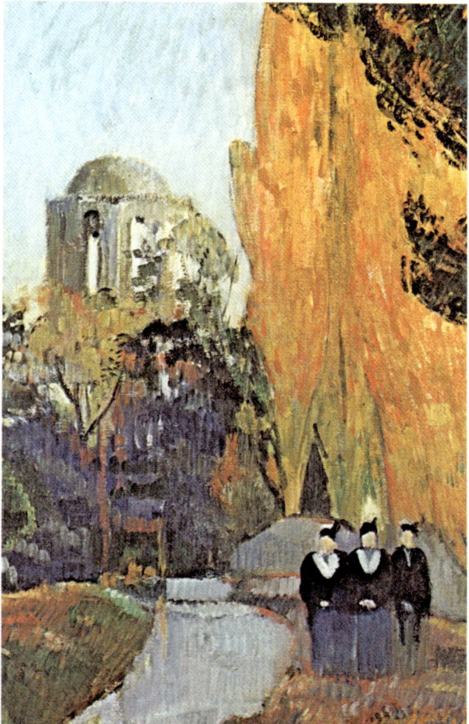

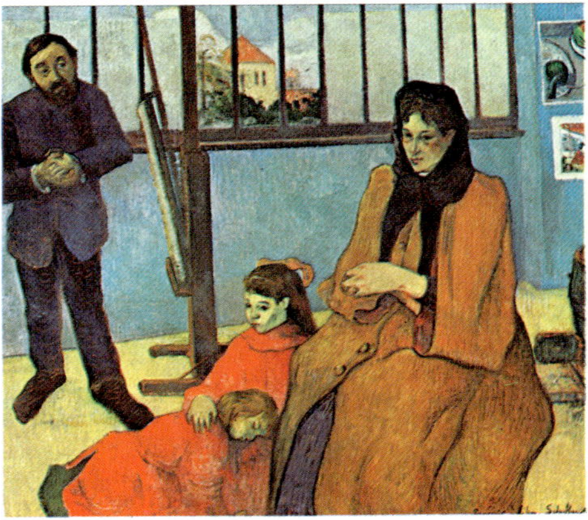

The Schuffenecker family and details (opposite and overleaf), 1889.
Oil on canvas, 73 × 92 cm ($28^{3}/_{4}$ × $36^{1}/_{4}$ in).
Paris, Musée d'Orsay.

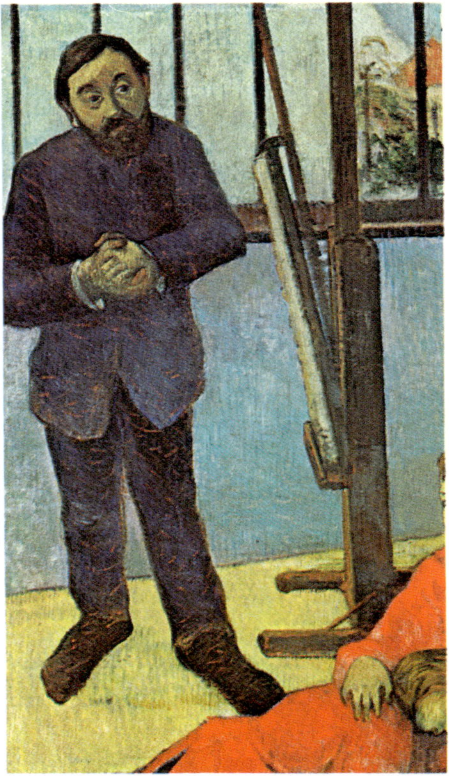

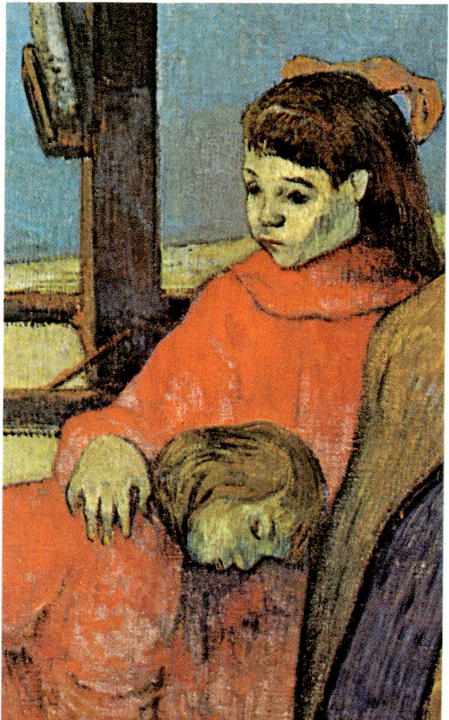

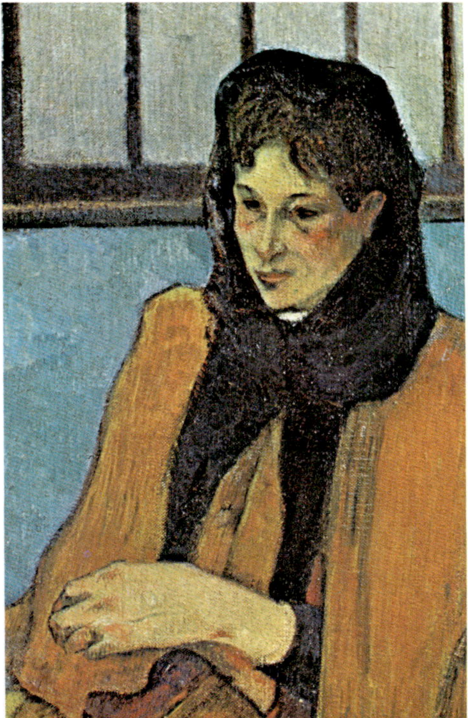

The yellow Christ and details (opposite and overleaf), 1889.
Oil on canvas, 92 × 73 cm ($36\frac{1}{4}$ × $28\frac{3}{4}$ in).
Buffalo, New York, Albright-Knox Art Gallery.

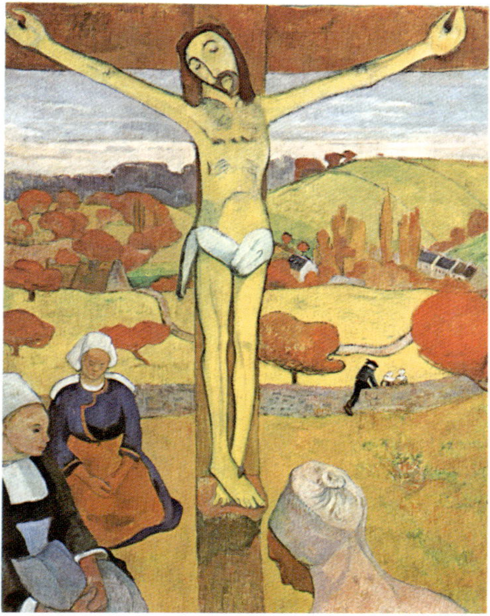

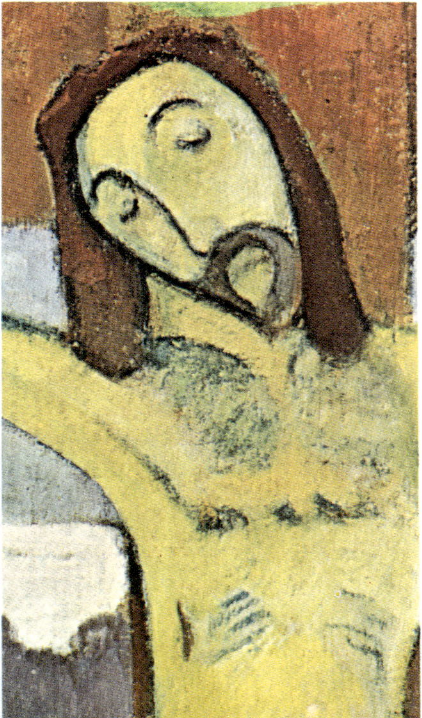

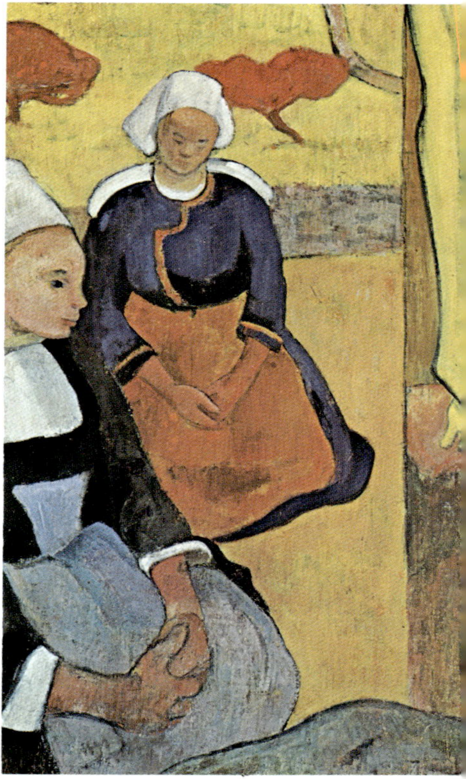

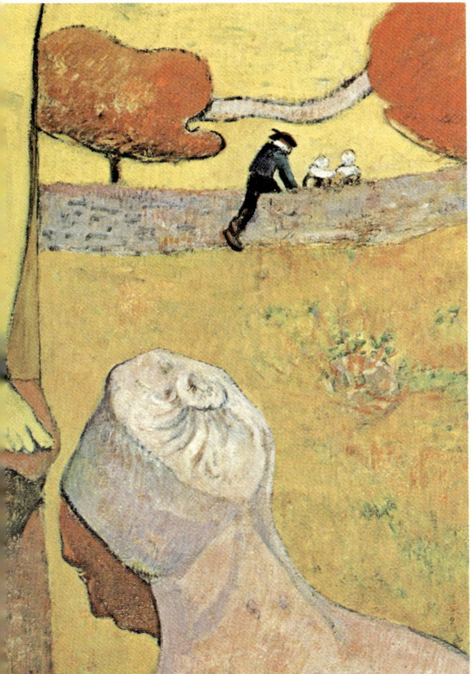
P Gauguin 89

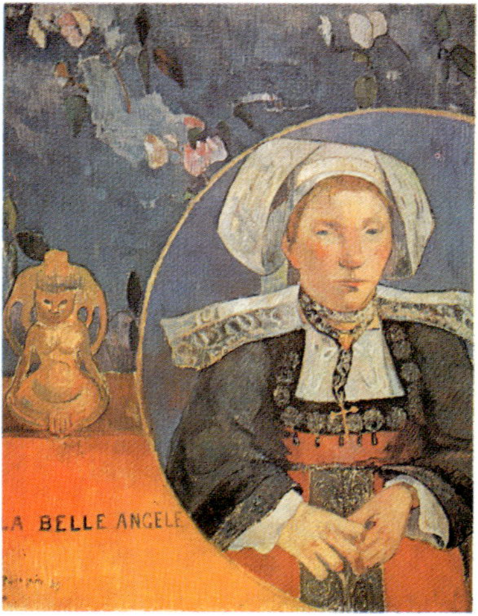

'La belle Angèle' (Portrait of Mme Satre) and details (opposite and overleaf), 1889.
Oil on canvas, 92×73 cm ($36\frac{1}{4} \times 28\frac{3}{4}$ in).
Paris, Musée d'Orsay.

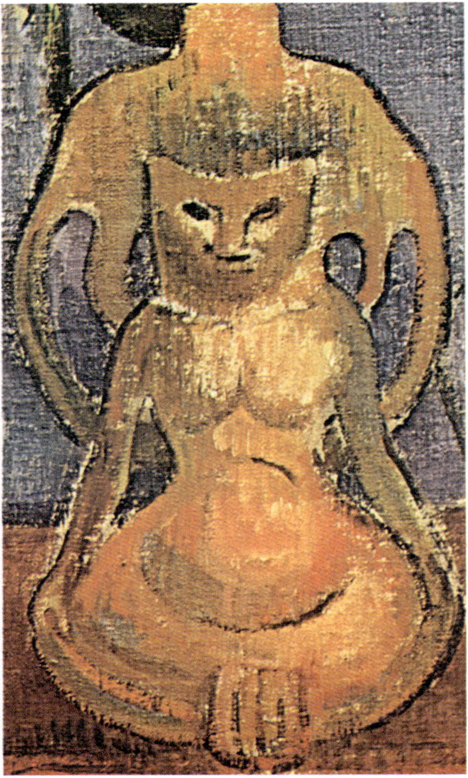

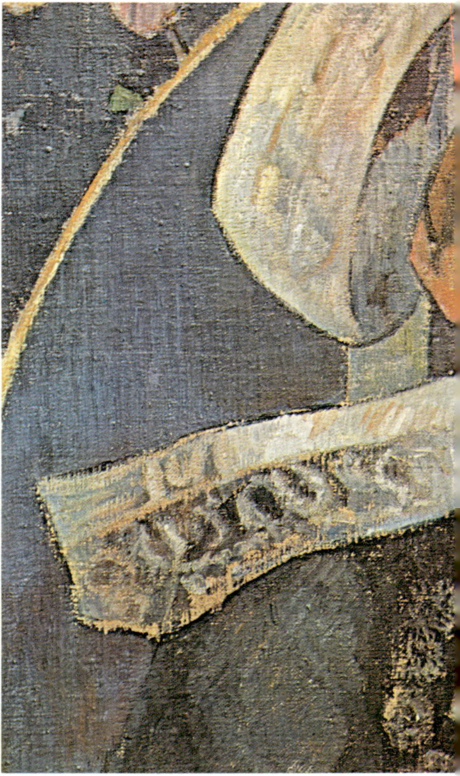

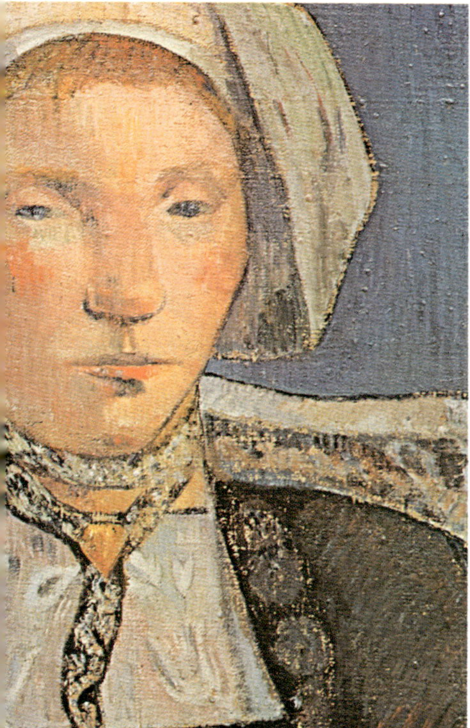

Still life with fan and detail (overleaf), 1889.

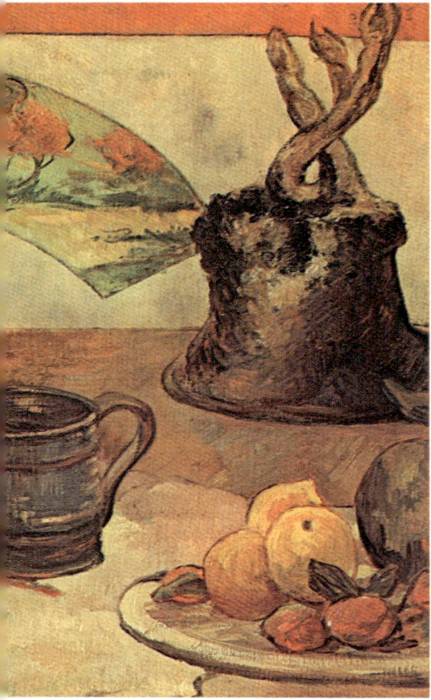

Oil on canvas, 50 × 61 cm (19⅝ × 24 in).
Paris, Musée d'Orsay.

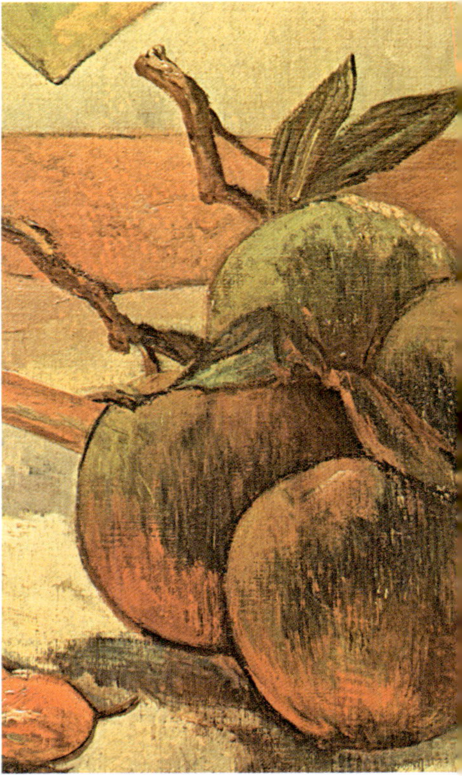

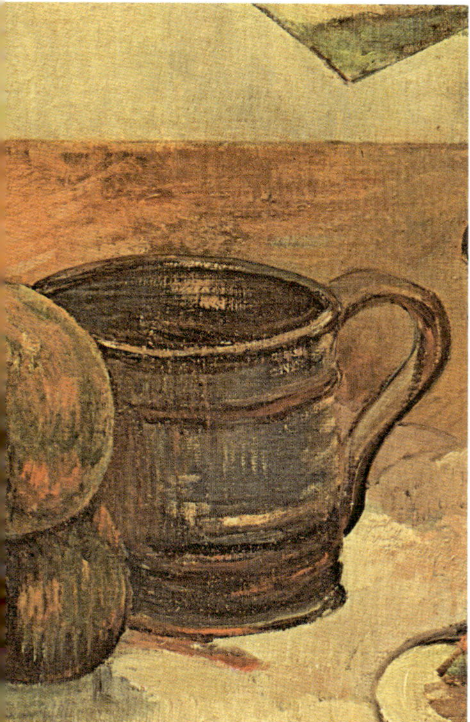

Aline Marie Chazal Gauguin (The artist's mother) 1889.
Oil on canvas, 41 × 33 cm
($16\frac{1}{8}$ × 13 in).
Stuttgart, Staatsgalerie.

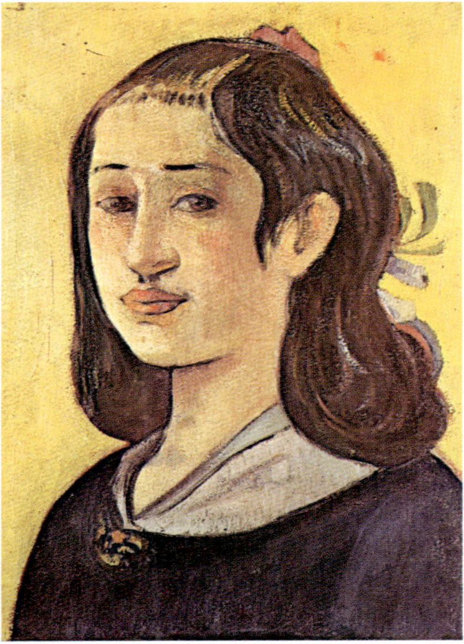

Farm at Le Pouldu 1890.
Oil on canvas, 73 × 92 cm (28¾ × 36¼ in).
Milan, private collection.

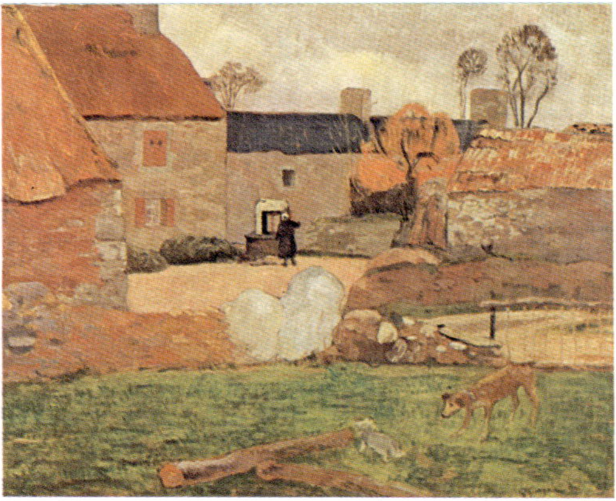

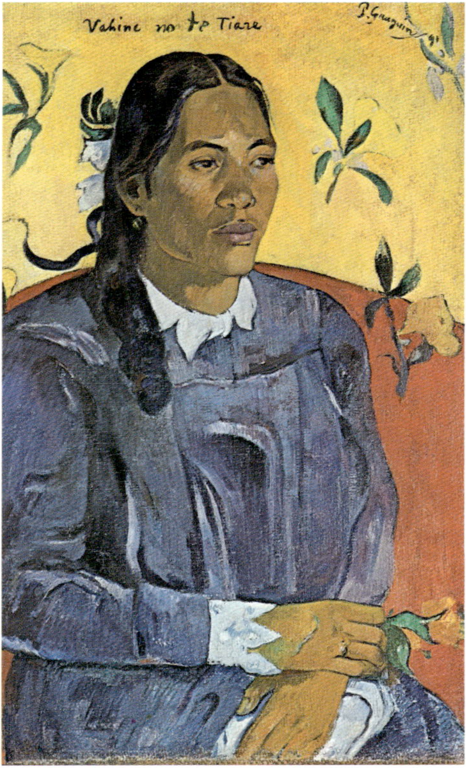
Vahine no te Tiare
P. Gauguin 91

'Vahine no te tiare' (Woman with a flower) and details (below and overleaf), 1891.
Oil on canvas, 70.5 × 46.5 cm ($27\frac{3}{4} \times 18\frac{1}{4}$ in).
Copenhagen, Ny Carlsberg Glyptotek.

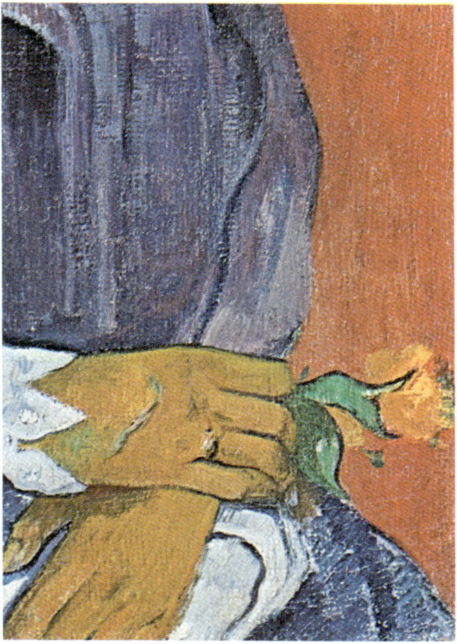

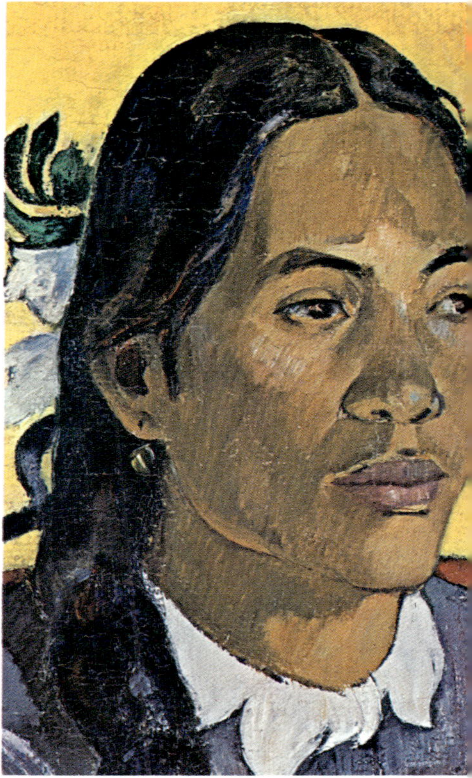

'Ia Orana Maria (Hail Mary) and details (opposite and overleaf), 1891.
Oil on canvas, 113.7 × 87.7 cm (44¾ × 34½ in).
New York, Metropolitan Museum of Art.

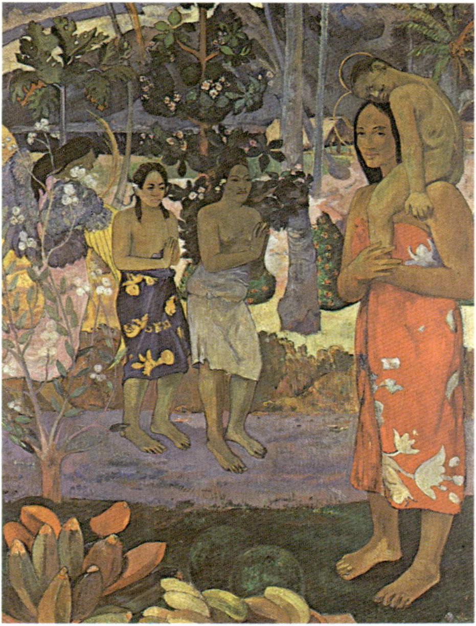

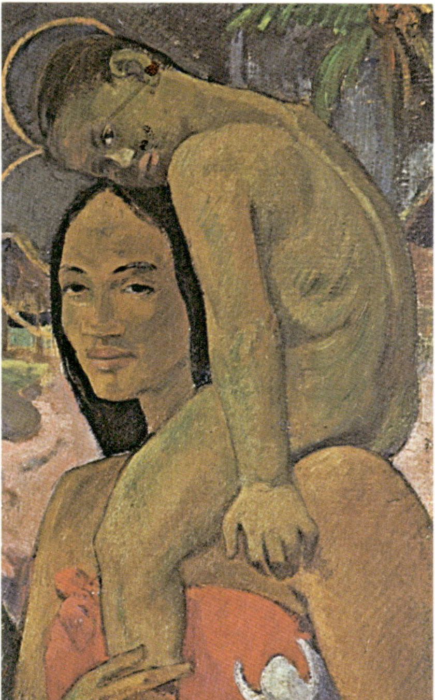

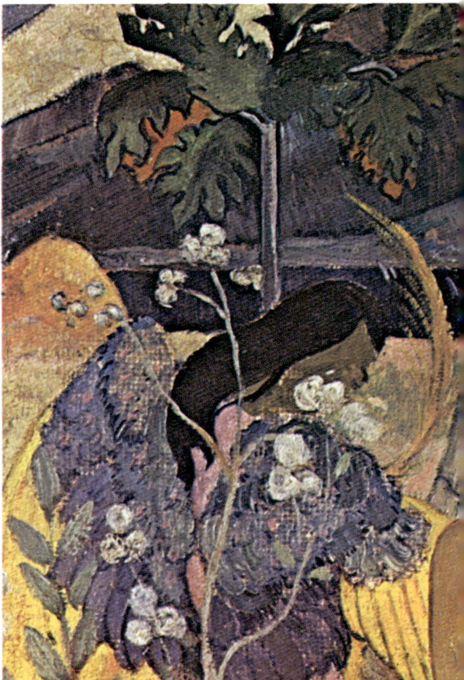

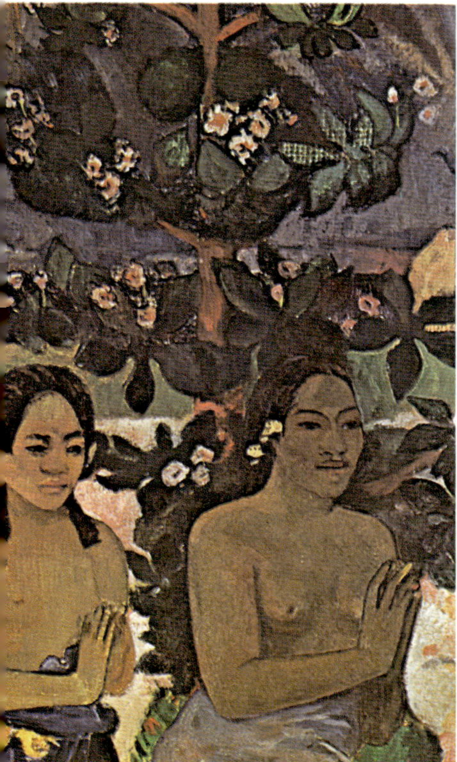

Two Tahitian women on the beach and details (overleaf), 1891.

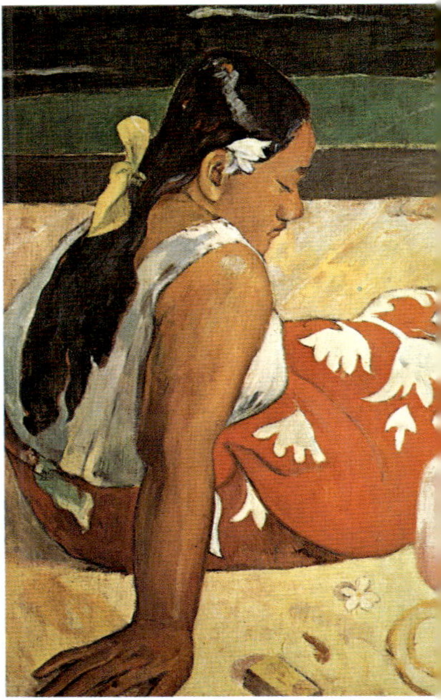

Oil on canvas, 69 × 90 cm ($27\frac{1}{8}$ × $35\frac{1}{2}$ in).
Paris, Musée d'Orsay.

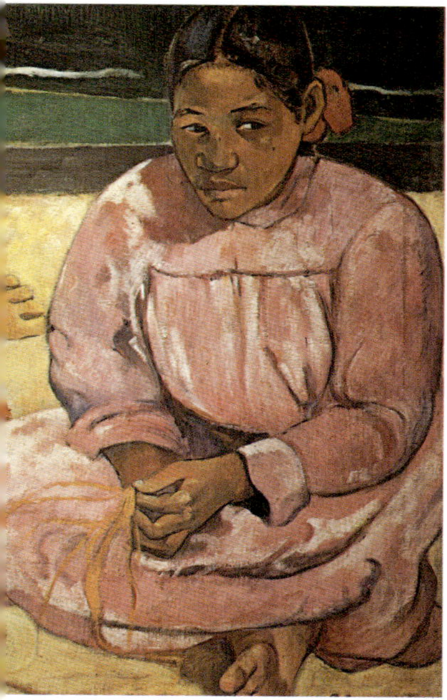

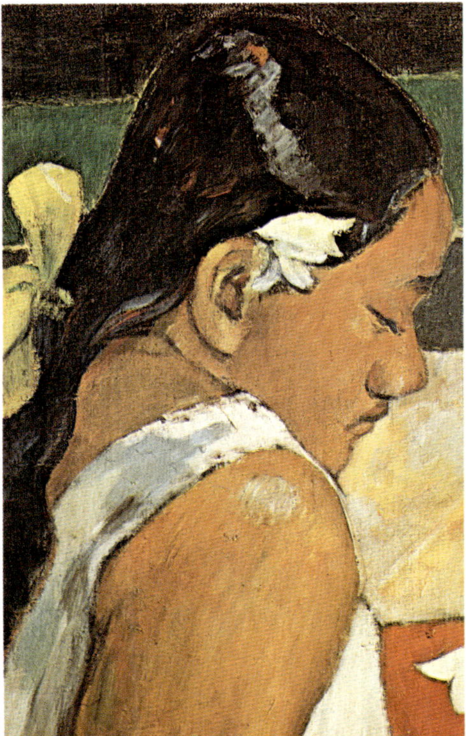

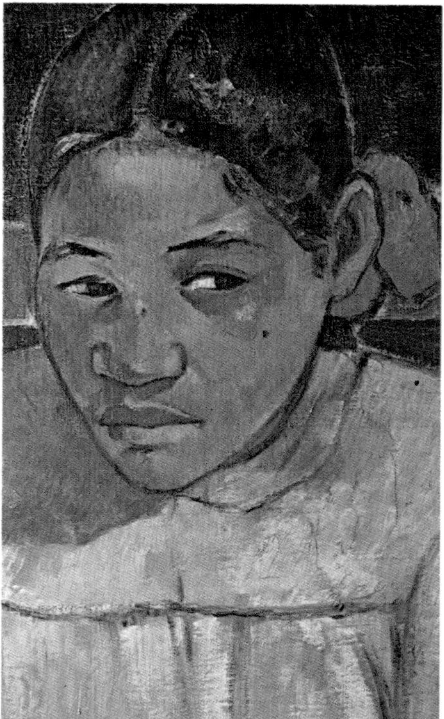

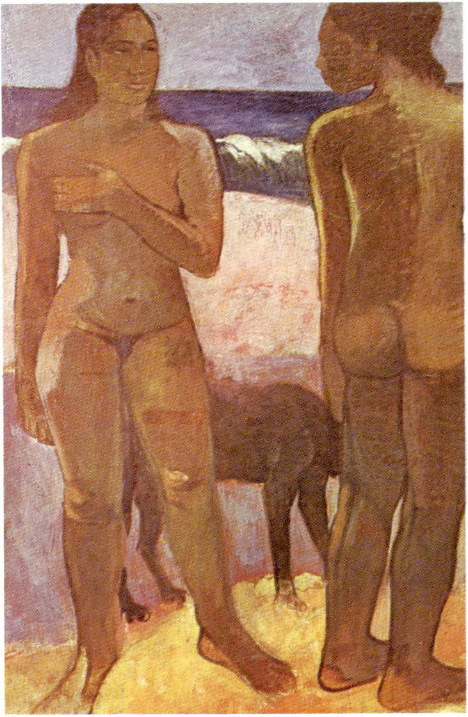

Two Tahitian women on the beach and detail (below), 1892?
Oil on canvas, 91 × 64 cm ($35\frac{7}{8}$ × $25\frac{1}{4}$ in).
Honolulu, Academy of Art.

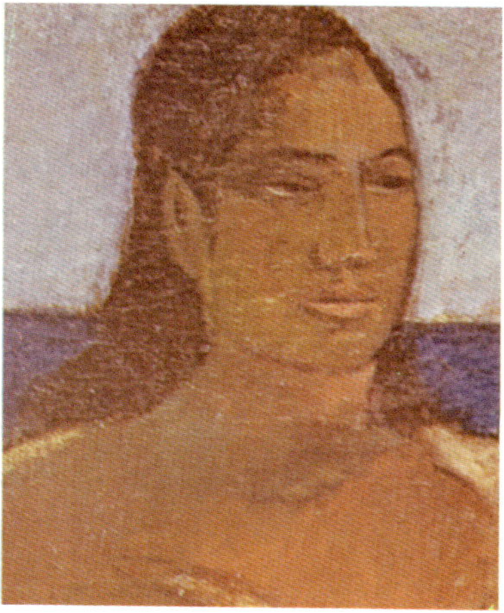

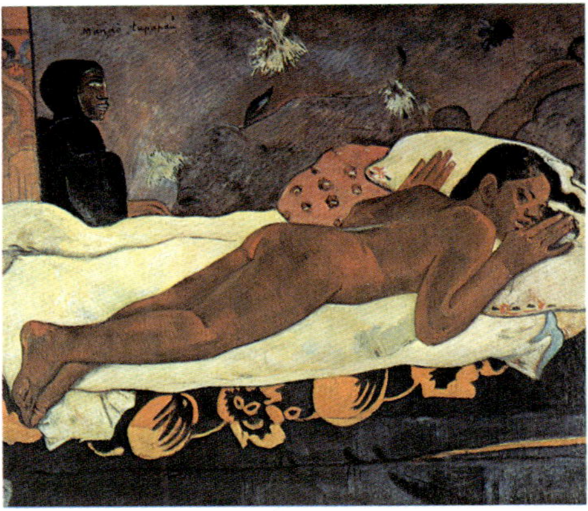

'Manau tupapau' (The spirit of the dead keeps watch) and details (opposite and overleaf), 1892.
Oil on canvas, 73 × 92 cm ($28\frac{3}{4}$ × $36\frac{1}{4}$ in).
Buffalo, New York, Albright-Knox Art Gallery.

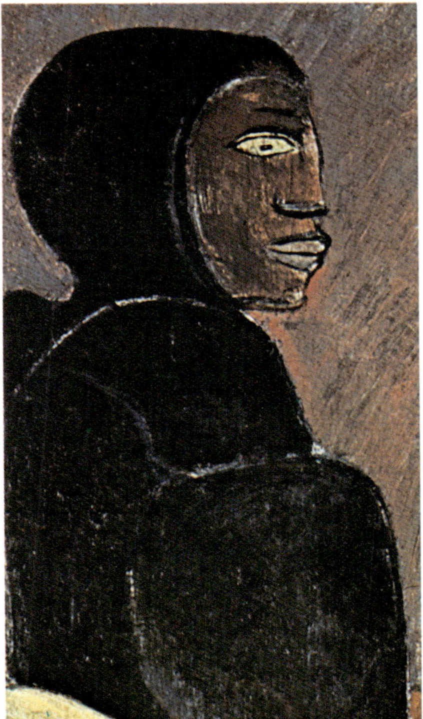

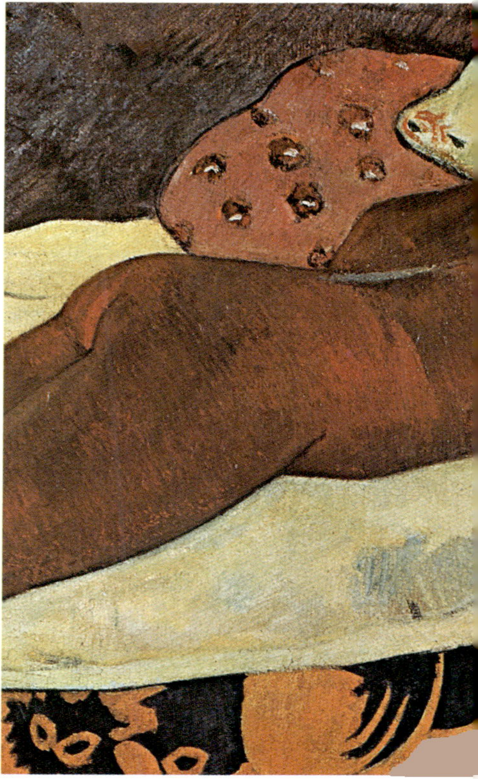

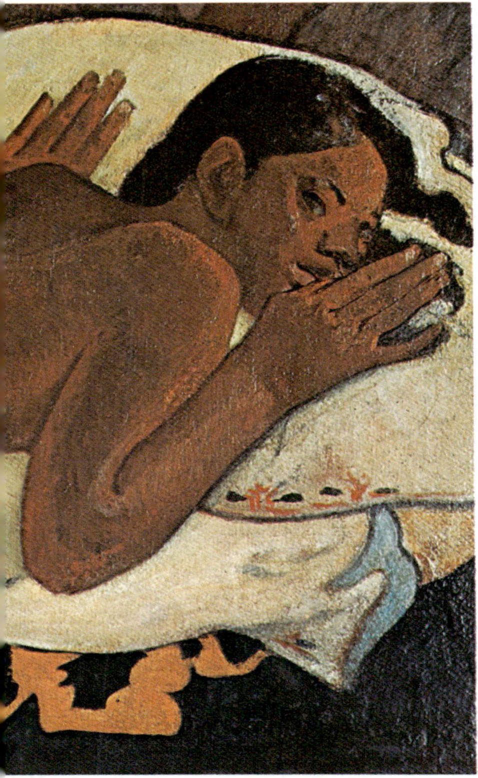

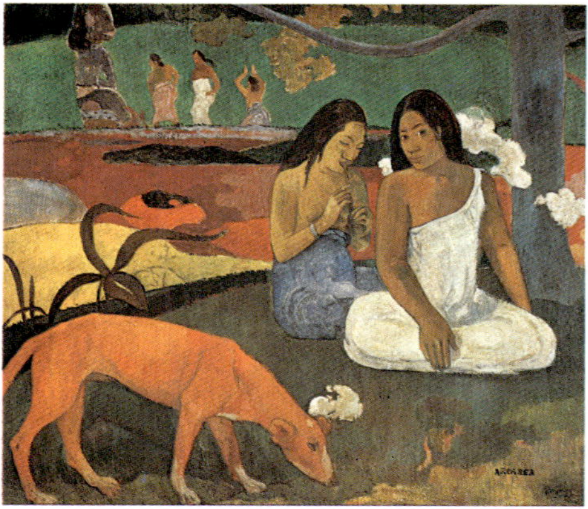

'Arearea' (Amusement) and details (opposite, overleaf and pages 96-97), 1892.
Oil on canvas, 75 × 94 cm ($29\frac{1}{2} \times 37$ in).
Paris, Musée d'Orsay.

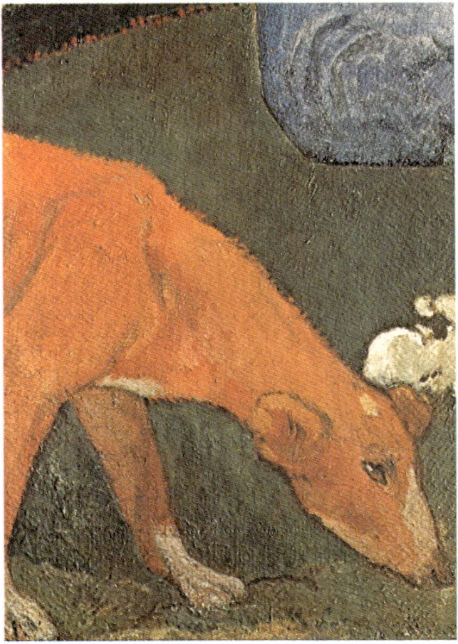

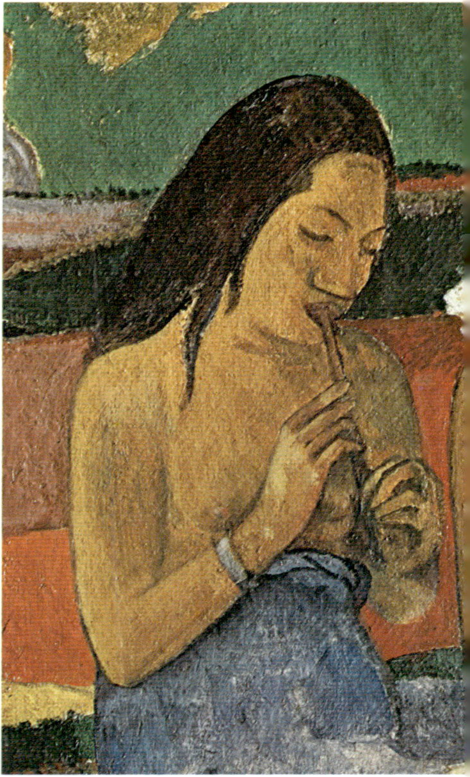

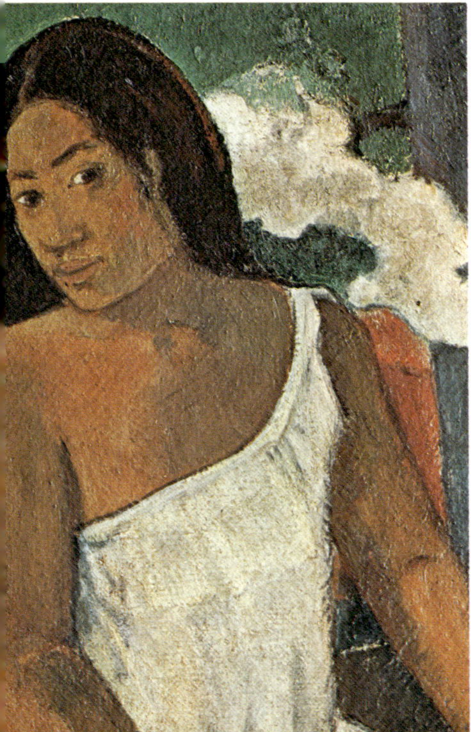

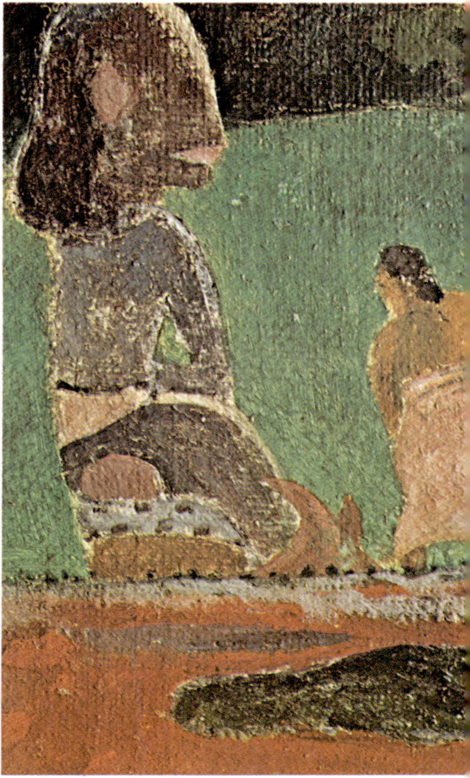

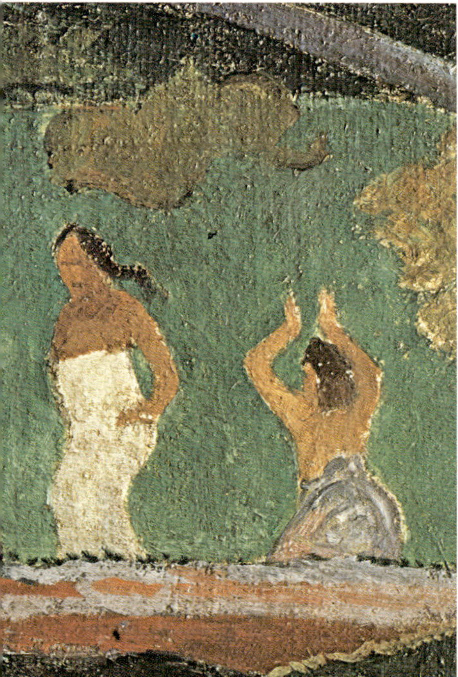

'Ta matete' (We shall not go to market today) and details (opposite and overleaf), 1982.
Oil on canvas, 73 × 91.5 cm (28¾ × 36¼ in).
Basle, Kunstmuseum.

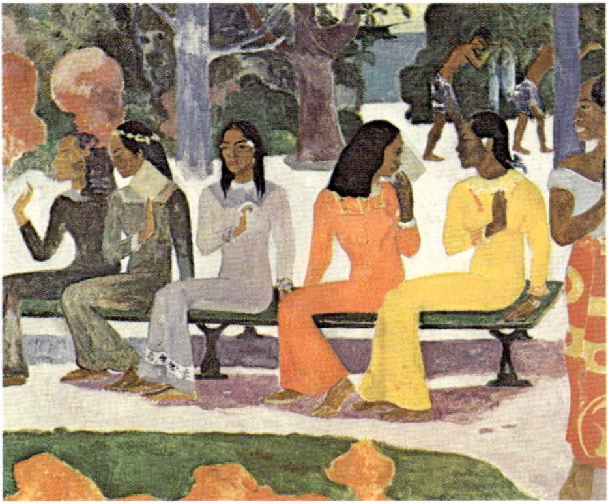

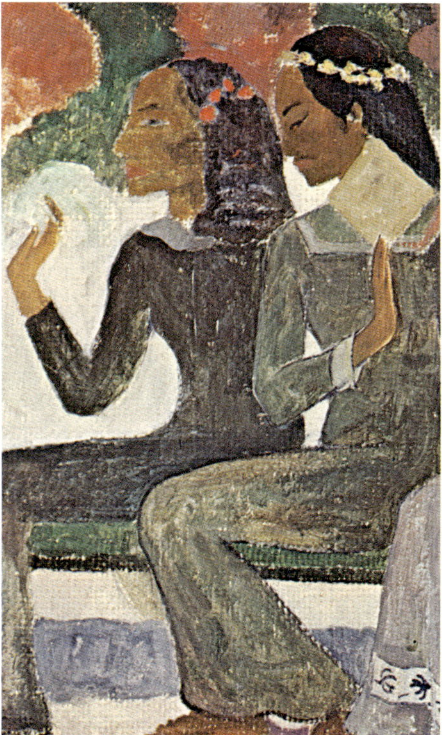

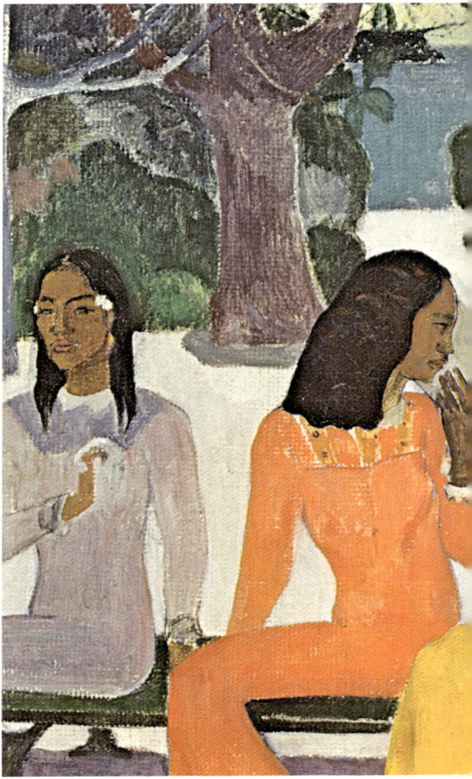

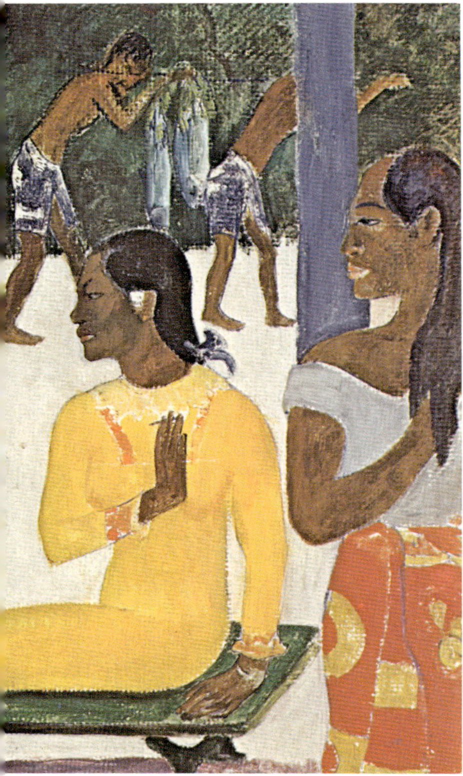

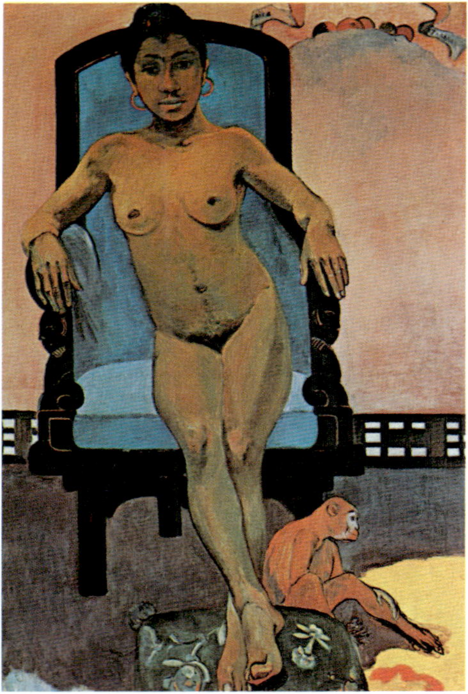

'Aita tamari vahine Judith te parari' (The child Judith has not yet been violated) or *Anna the Javanese* and detail (below), 1893-1894.
Oil on canvas, 116 × 81.5 cm ($45\frac{3}{4}$ × 32 in).
Berne, private collection.

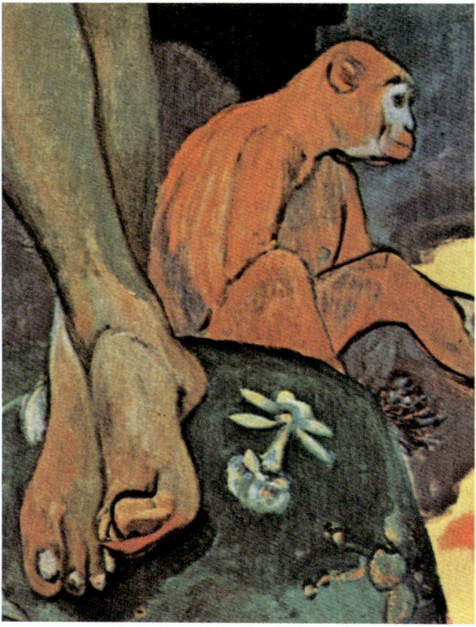

Self-portrait, wearing a hat and detail (opposite), 1893-1894.
Oil on canvas, 46 × 38 cm ($18\frac{1}{8}$ × 15 in).
Paris, Musée d'Orsay.

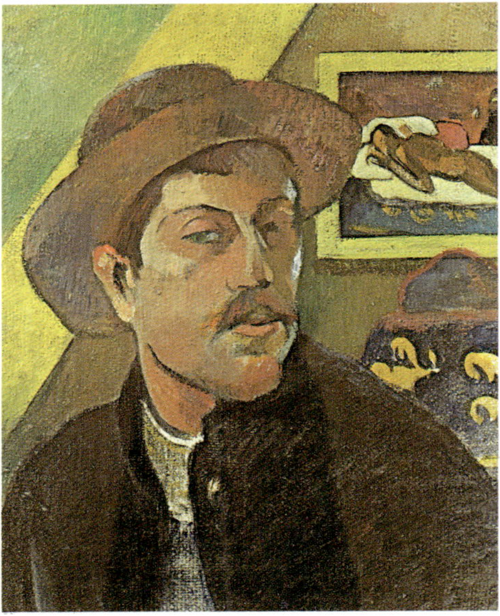

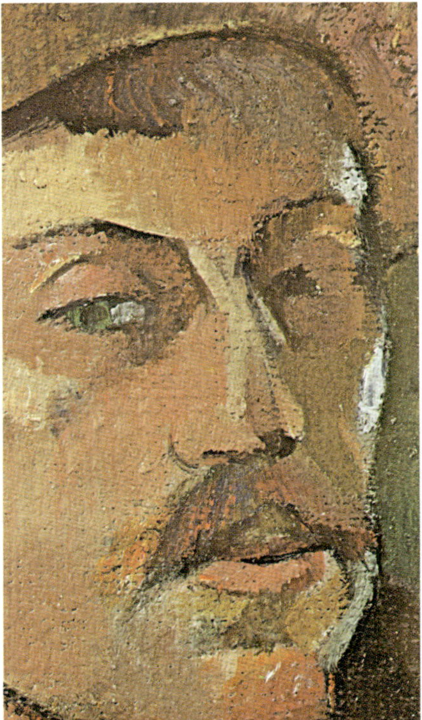

'Mahana no atua' (Day of God) and detail (opposite), 1894.
Oil on canvas, 69.6 × 90.5 cm ($27^3/_8$ × $35^3/_8$ in).
Chicago, Art Institute.

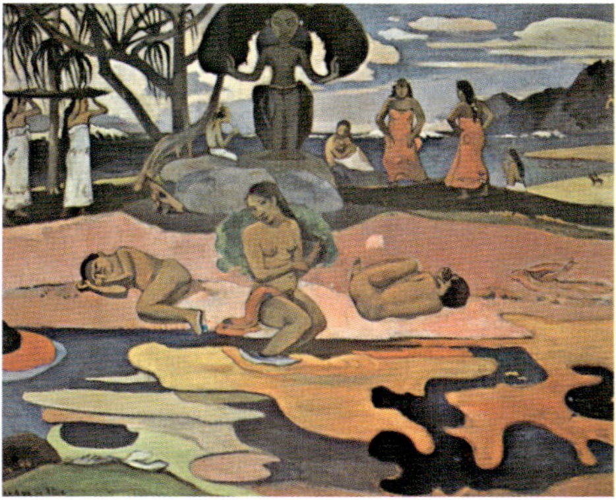

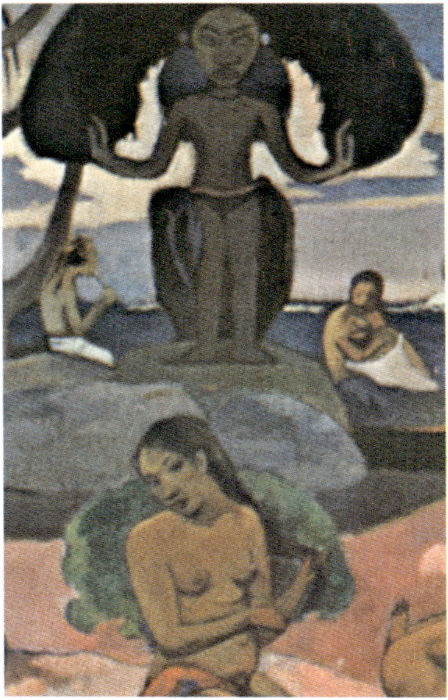

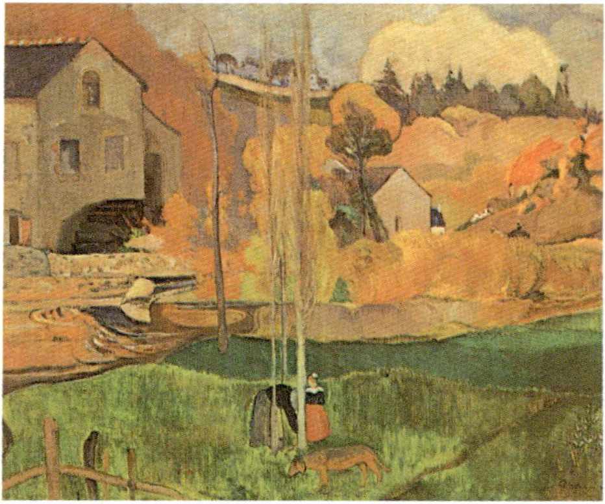

David's mill at Pont-Aven and detail (opposite), 1894.
Oil on canvas, 73 × 92 cm ($28^3/_4$ × $36^1/_4$ in).
Paris, Musée d'Orsay.

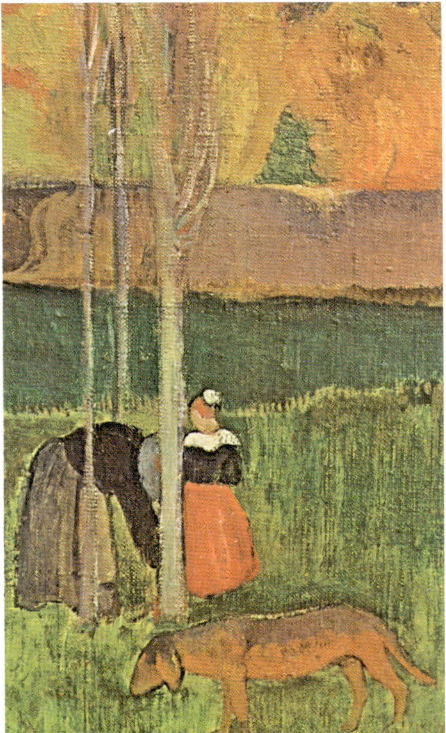

Christmas night and details (opposite and overleaf), 1894.
Oil on canvas, 72 × 83 cm ($28\frac{3}{8} \times 32\frac{5}{8}$ in).
New York, private collection.

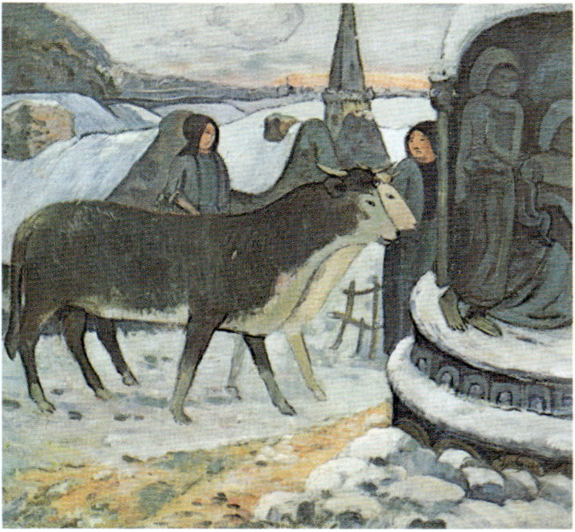

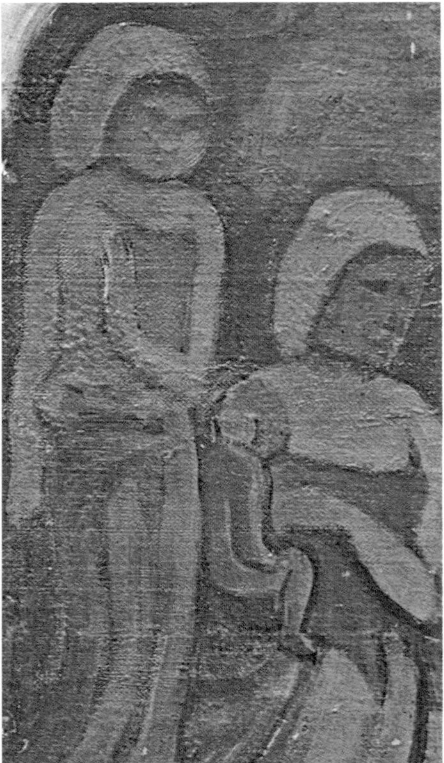

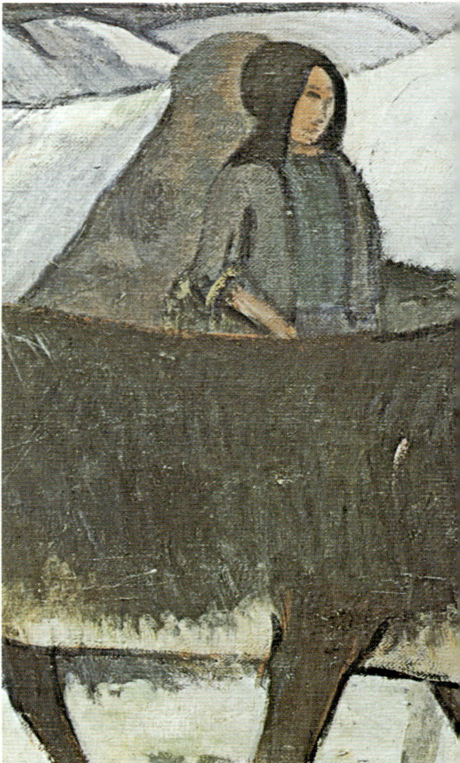

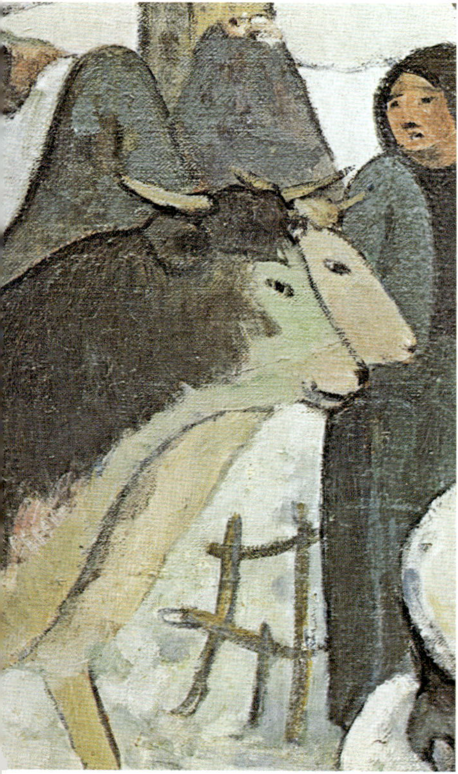

Village in the snow 1894.
Oil on canvas, 65 × 90 cm
(25⅝ × 35½ in).
Paris, Musée d'Orsay.

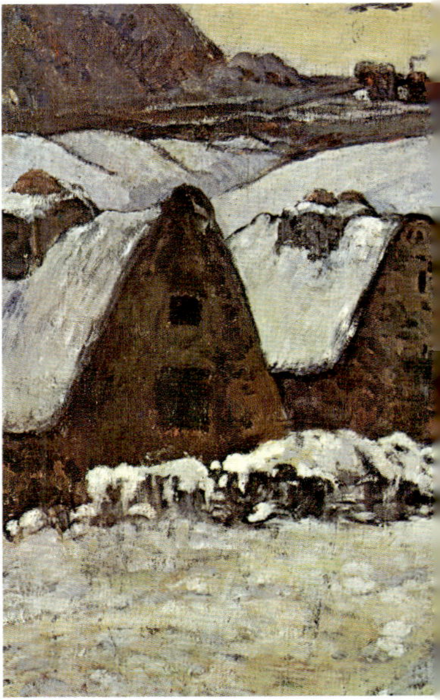

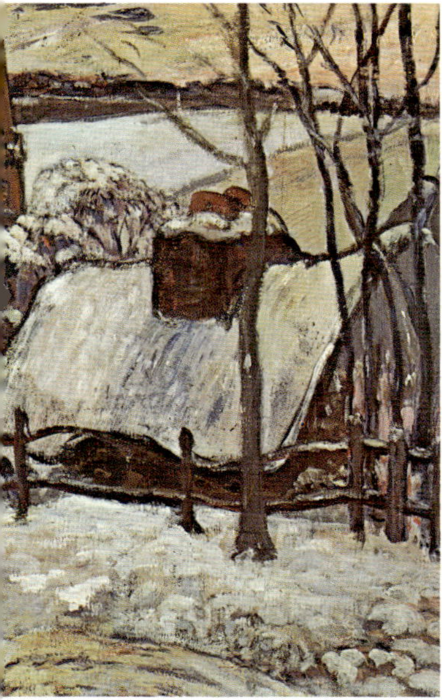

'Te tamari no atua' (The birth of Christ)
and detail (overleaf), 1896.
Oil on canvas, 96 × 128 cm
($37\frac{3}{4} \times 50\frac{3}{8}$ in).
Munich, Neue Pinakothek.

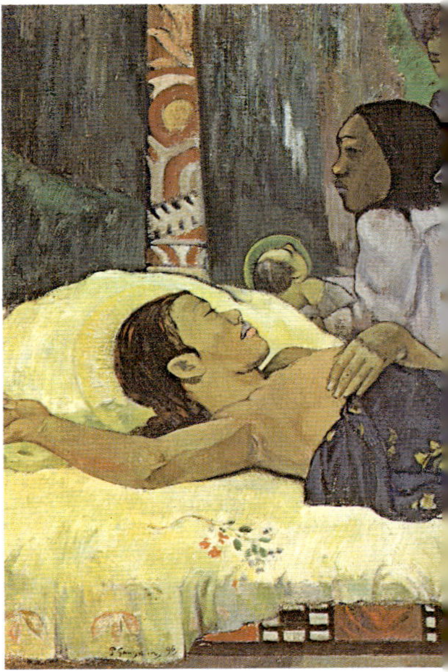

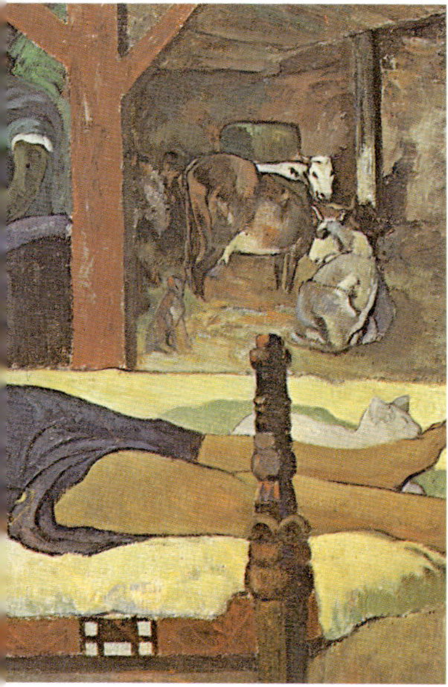

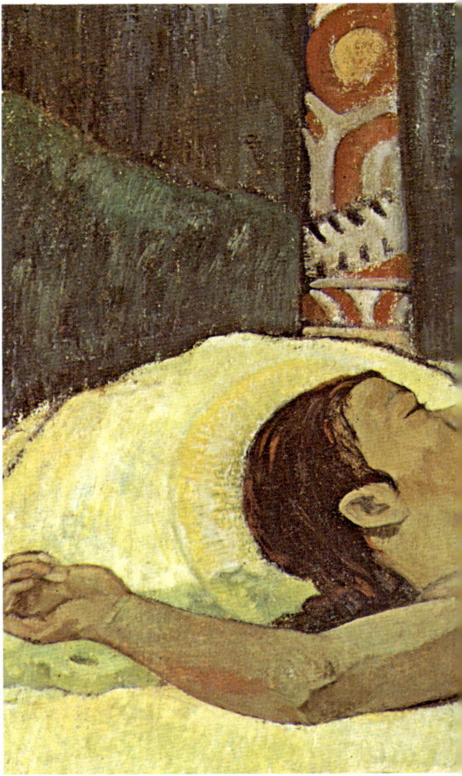

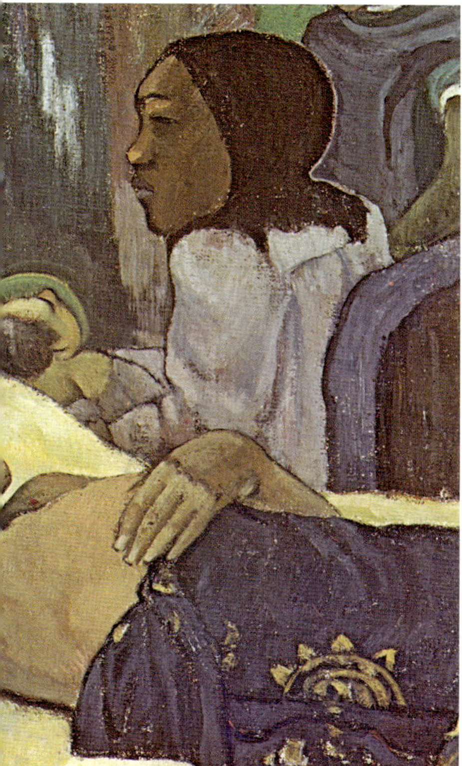

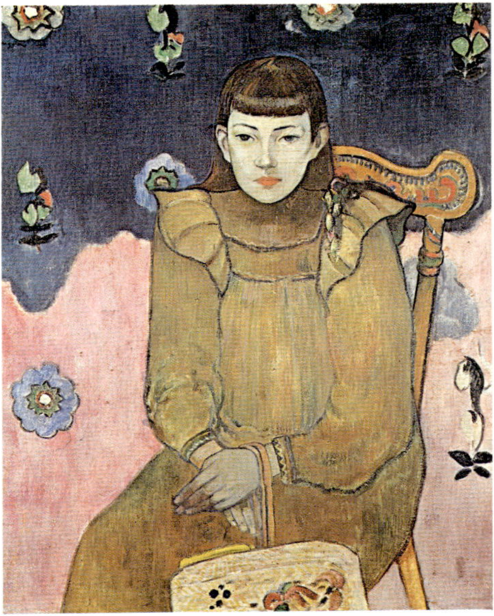

Vaite Goupil (Jeanne Goupil) and details (below and overleaf), 1896.
Oil on canvas, 75 × 65 cm (29½ × 25⅝ in).
Copenhagen, Ordrupgaard Collection.

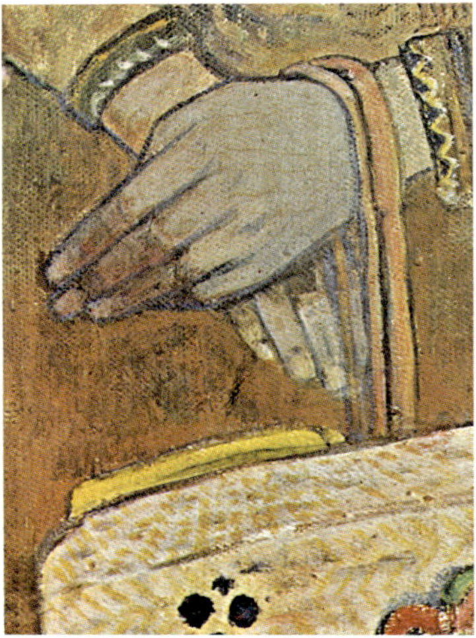

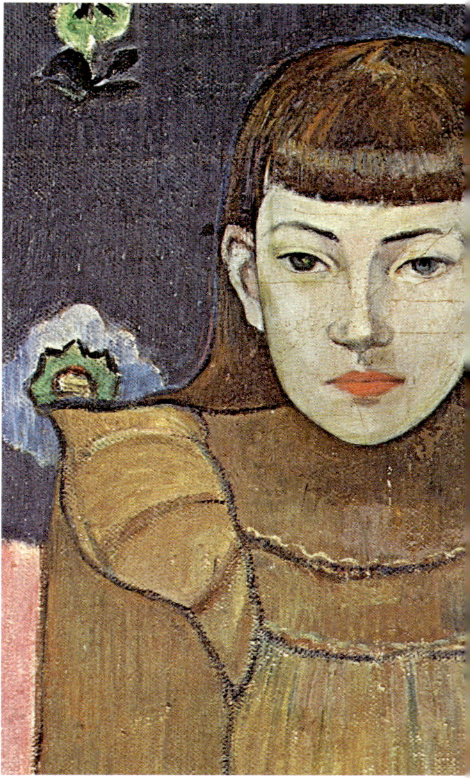

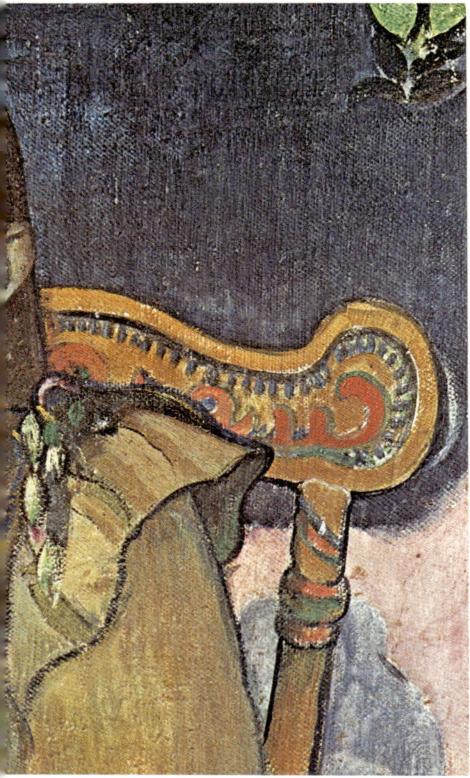

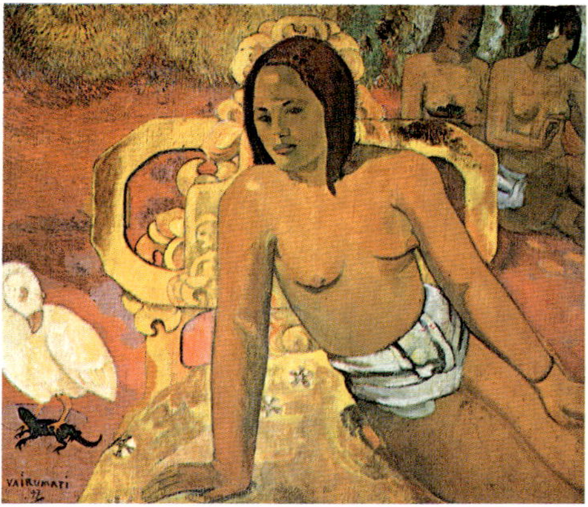

'Vairaoumati' (The earthly bride of the god Oro) and details (opposite and overleaf), 1897.
Oil on canvas, 73 × 94 cm (28¾ × 37 in).
Paris, Musée d'Orsay.

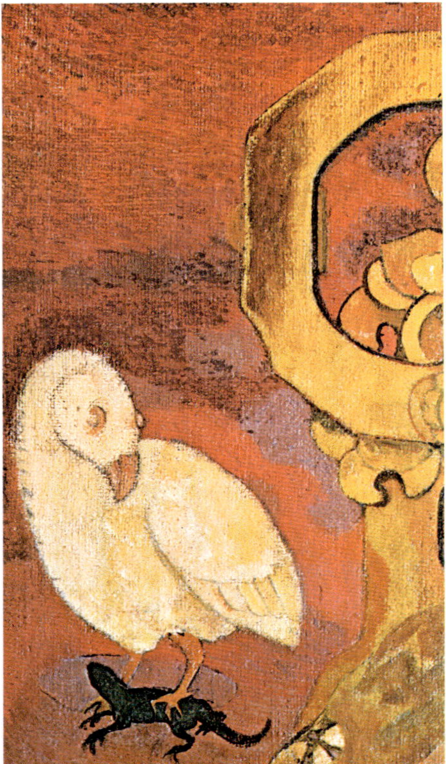

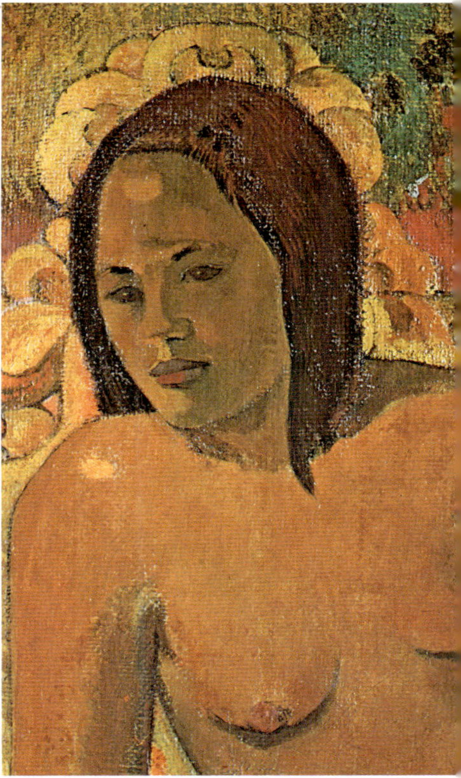

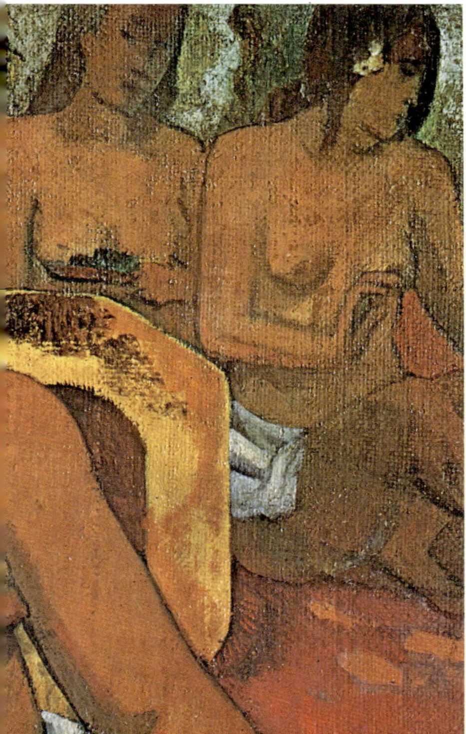

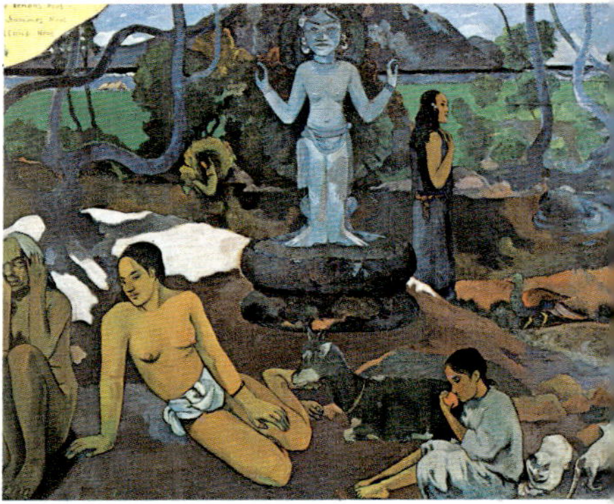

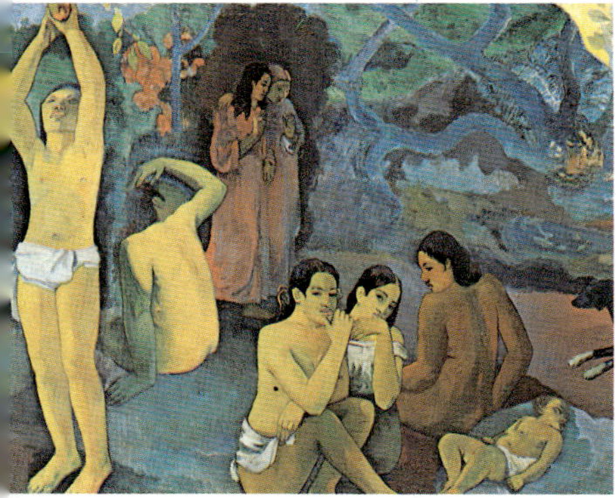

'D'Où venons-nous? Que sommes-nous? Où allons-nous?' (Where are we from? What are we? Where are we going?) and details (overleaf and pages 132-133, 134, 135, 136-137), 1897.
Oil on canvas, 139.1 × 374.6 cm ($54\frac{3}{4} \times 147\frac{1}{2}$ in).
Boston, Museum of Fine Arts.

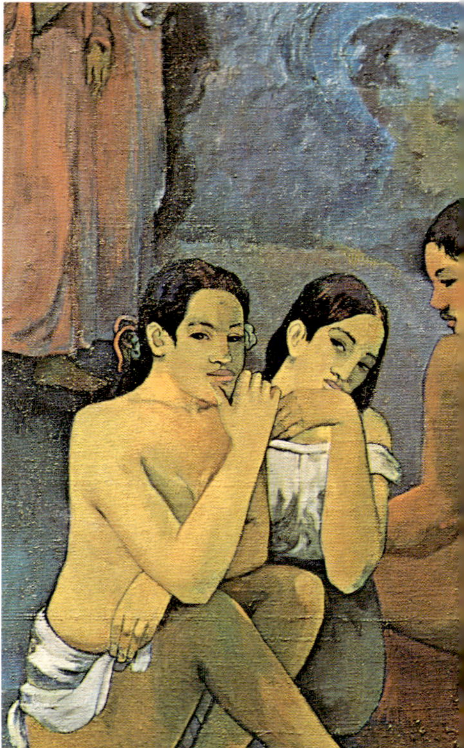

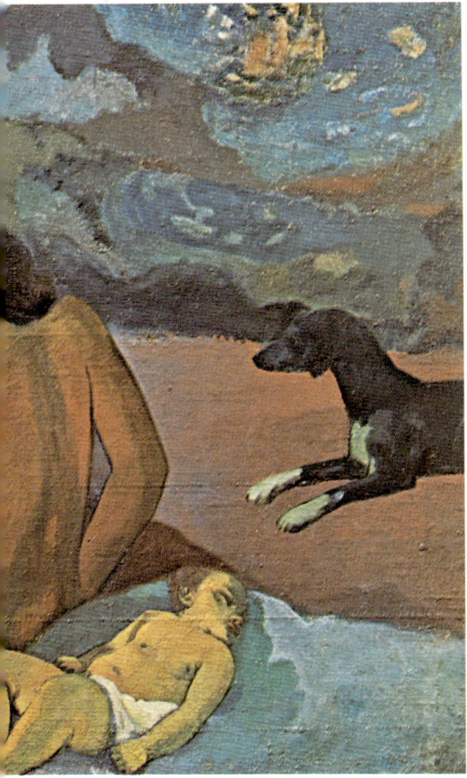

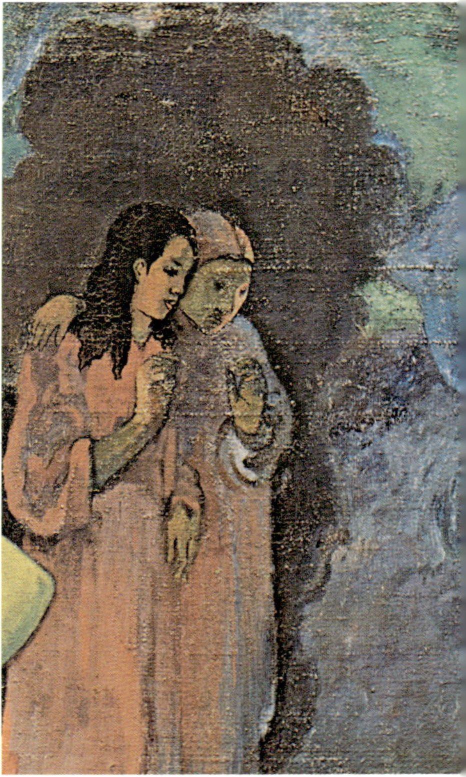

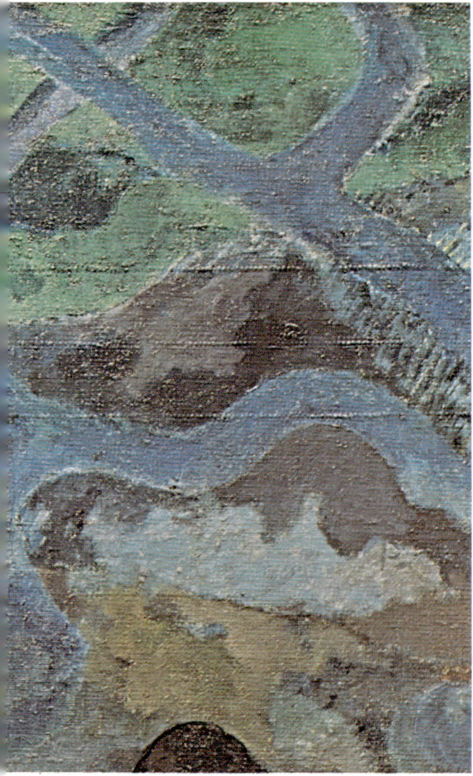

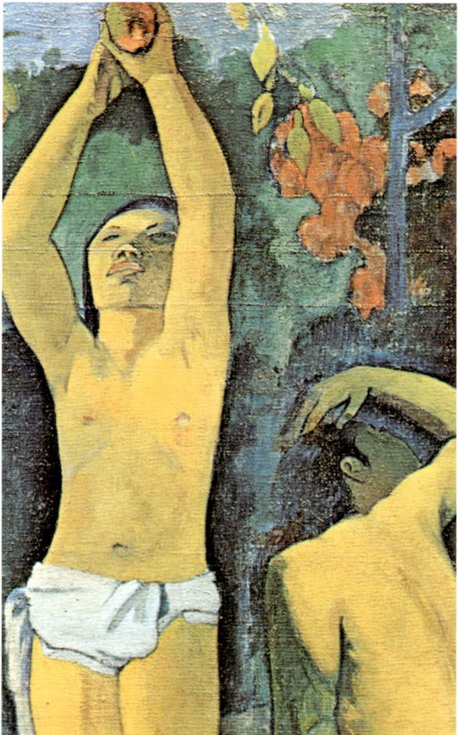

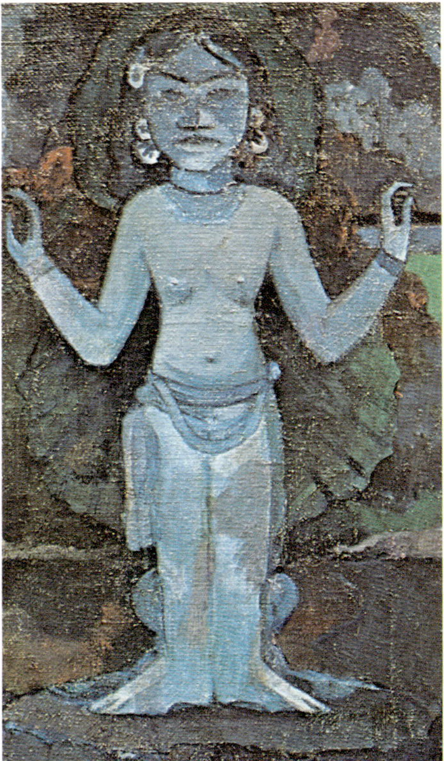

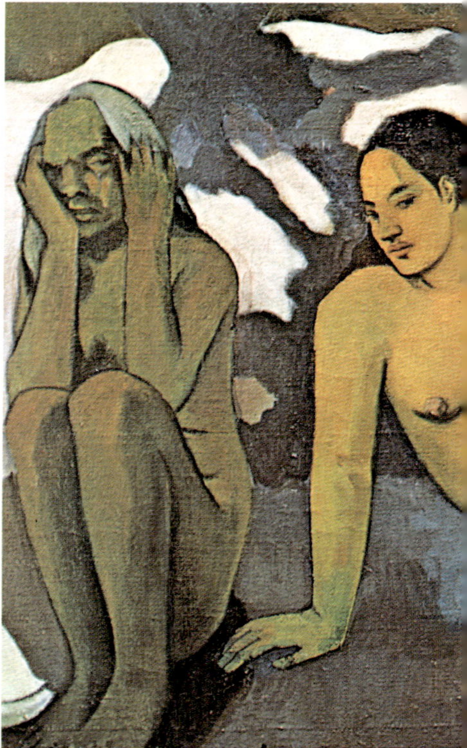

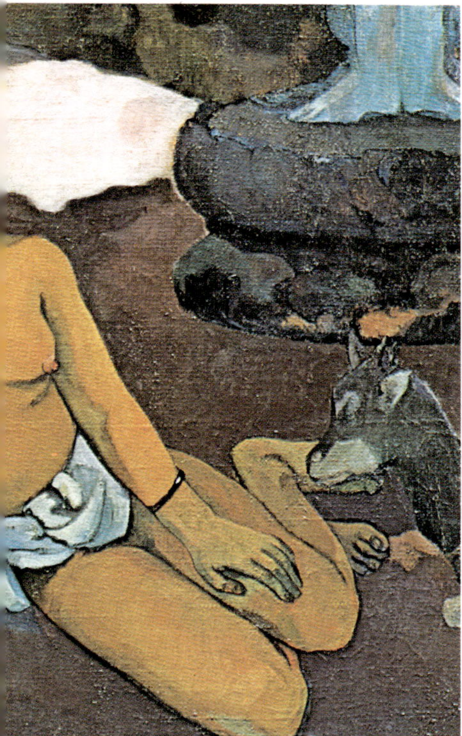

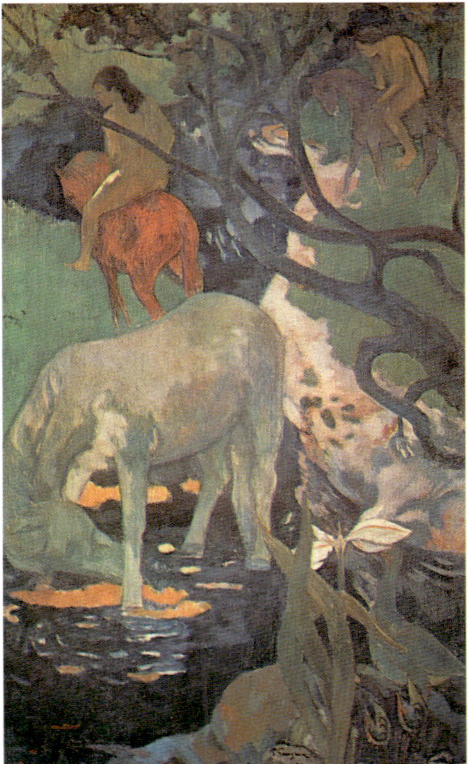

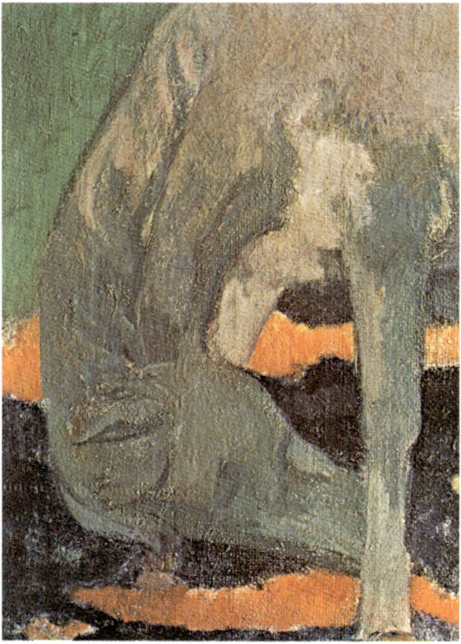

The white horse and details (below and overleaf), 1898.
Oil on canvas, 140 × 91.5 cm ($55\frac{1}{8}$ × 36 in).
Paris, Musée d'Orsay.

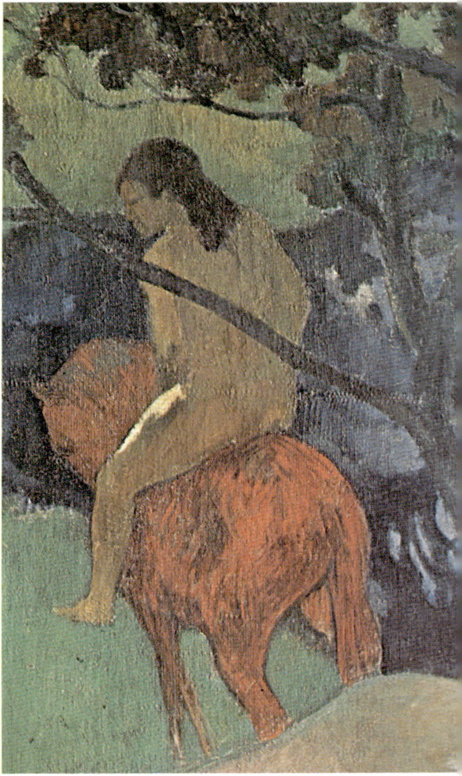

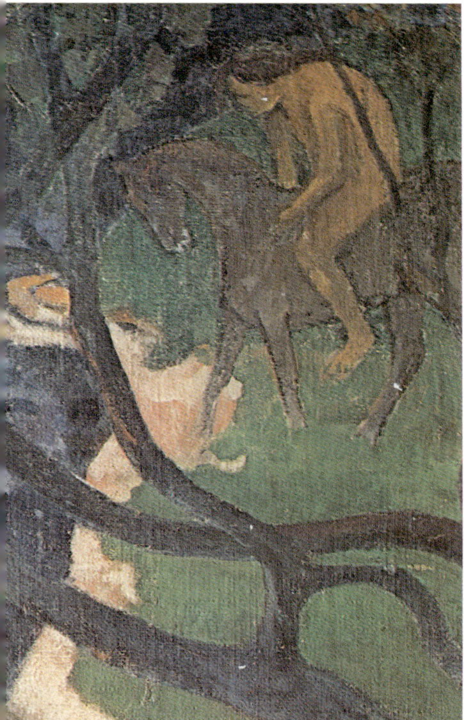

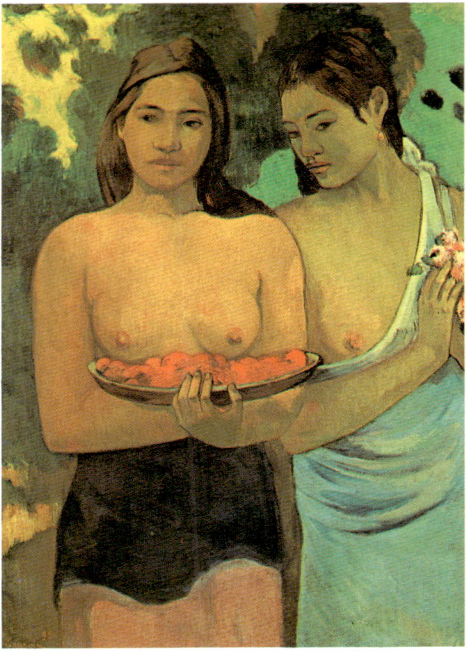

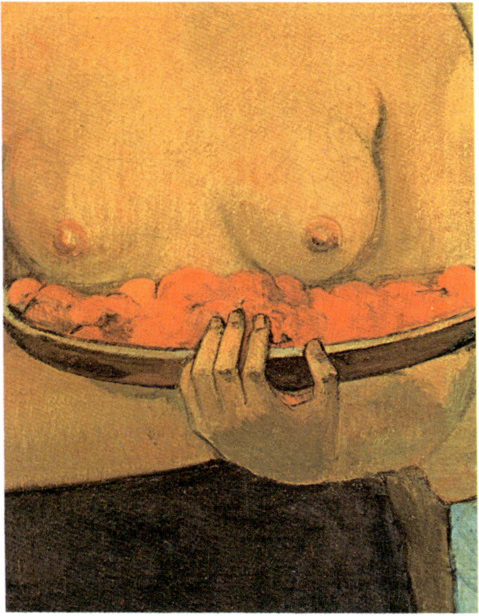

Two Tahitian women ('Les seins aux fleurs rouges')
and details (above and overleaf), 1899.
Oil on canvas, 94 × 73 cm (37 × 28¾ in).
New York, Metropolitan Musem of Art.

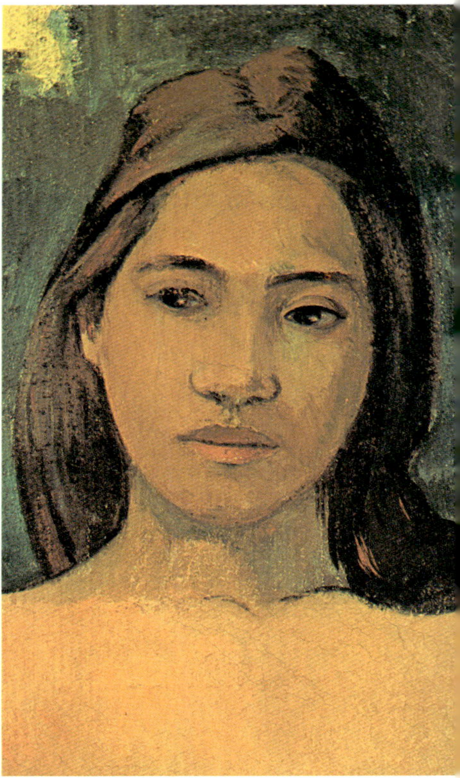

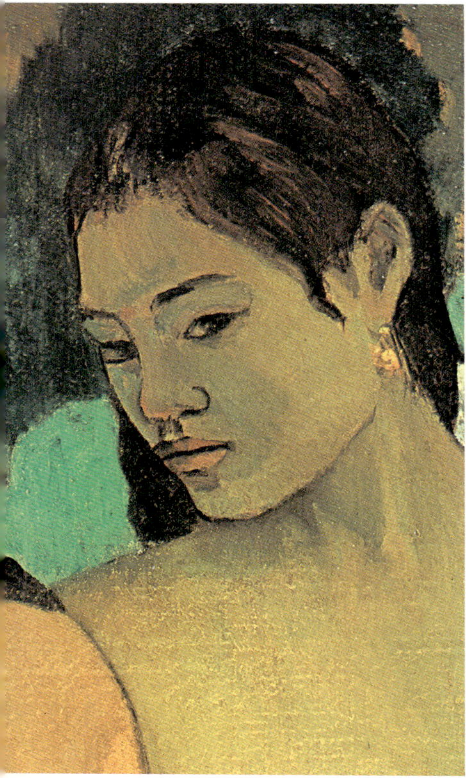

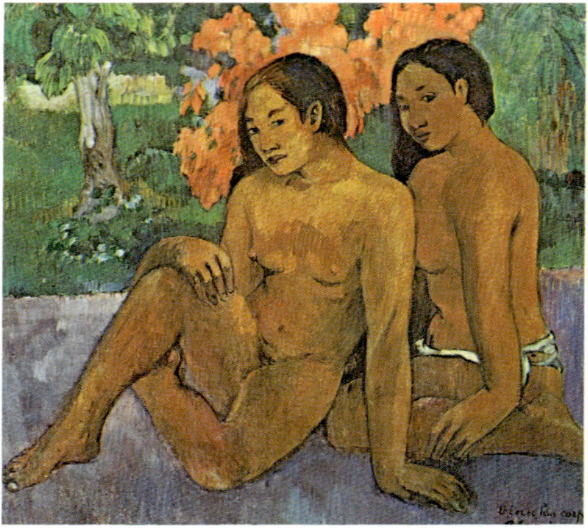

And the gold of their bodies and details (opposite and overleaf), 1901.
Oil on canvas, 67 × 76 cm ($26\frac{3}{8}$ × 30 in).
Paris, Musée d'Orsay.

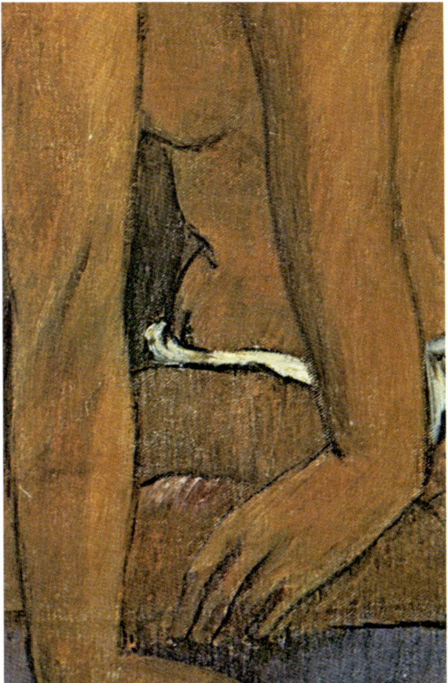

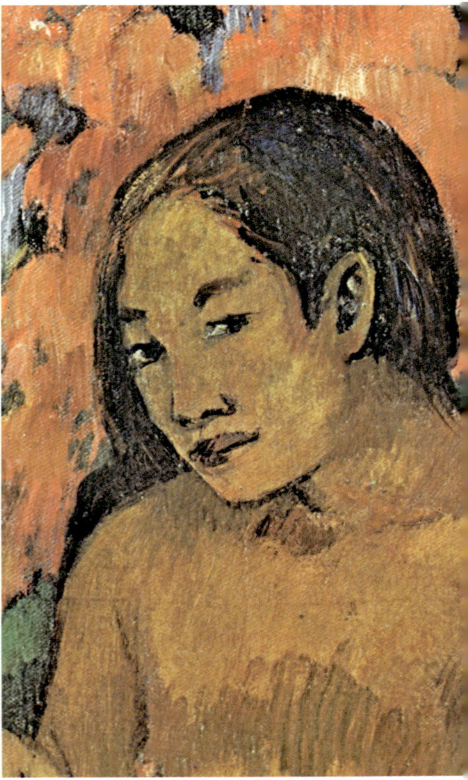

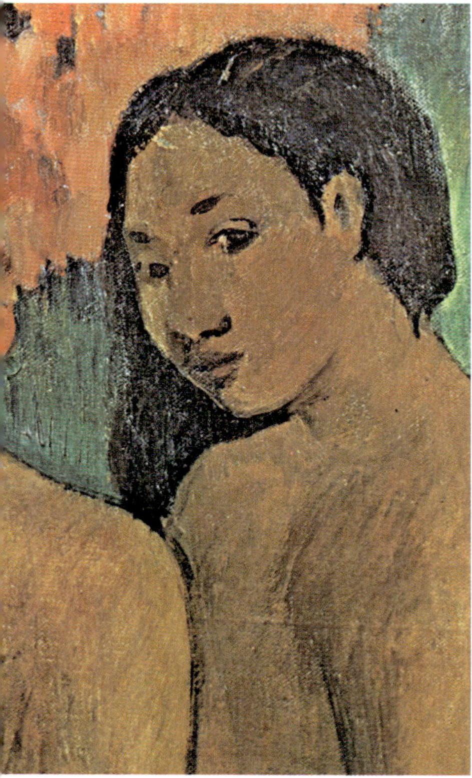

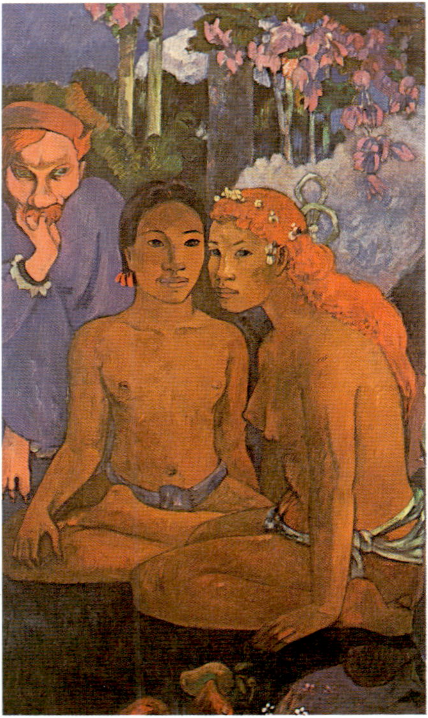

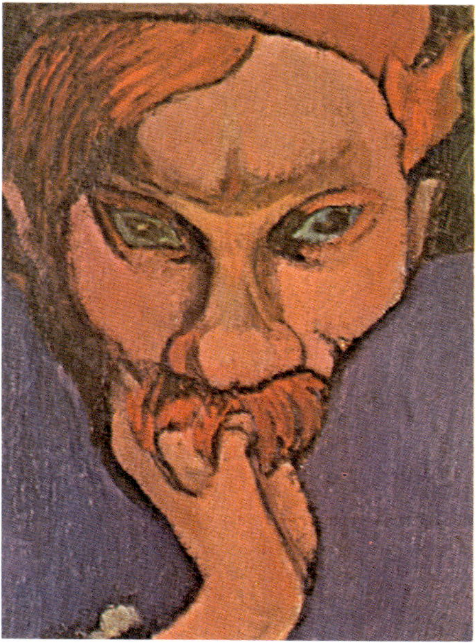

'Contes barbares' (Barbarous tales) and details (above, overleaf and pages 154-155), 1902. Oil on canvas, 130 × 89 cm (51⅛ × 35 in). Essen, Folkwang Museum.

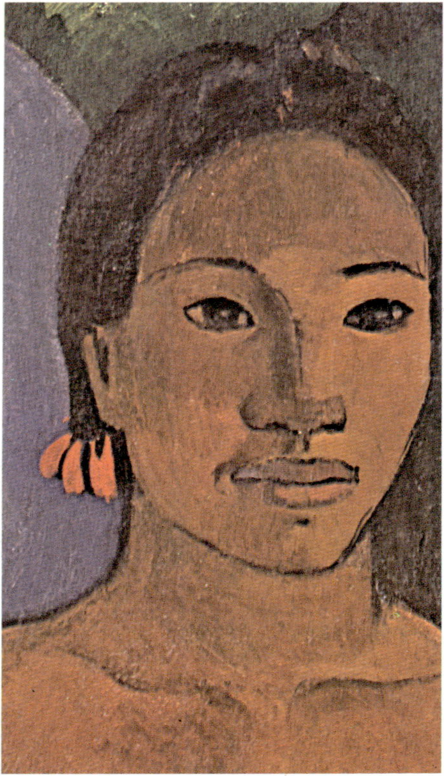

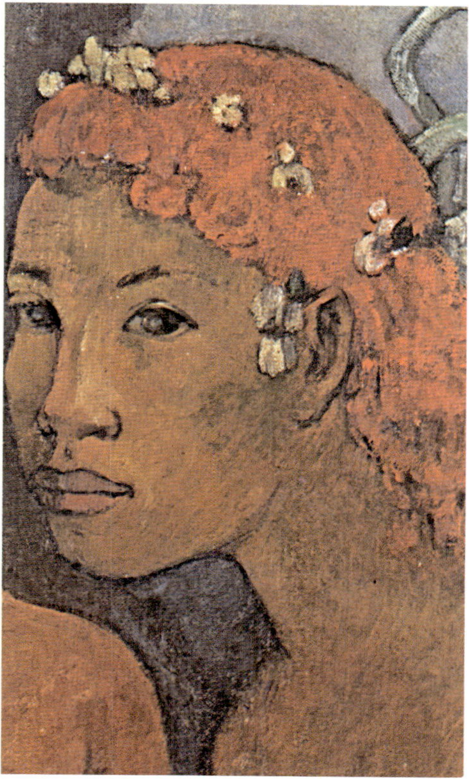

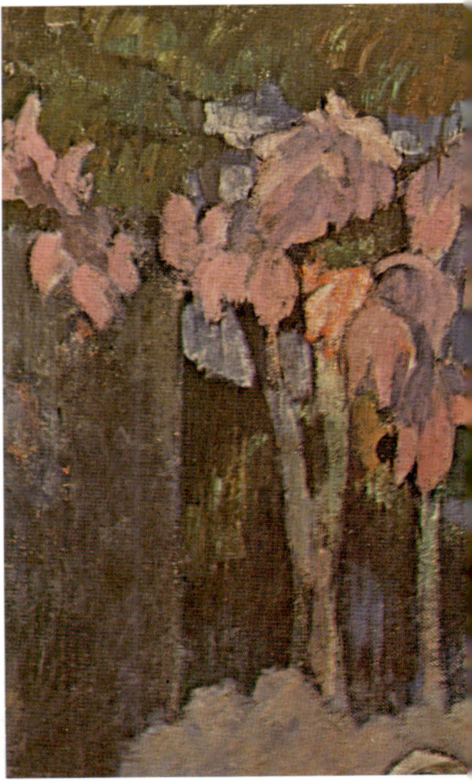

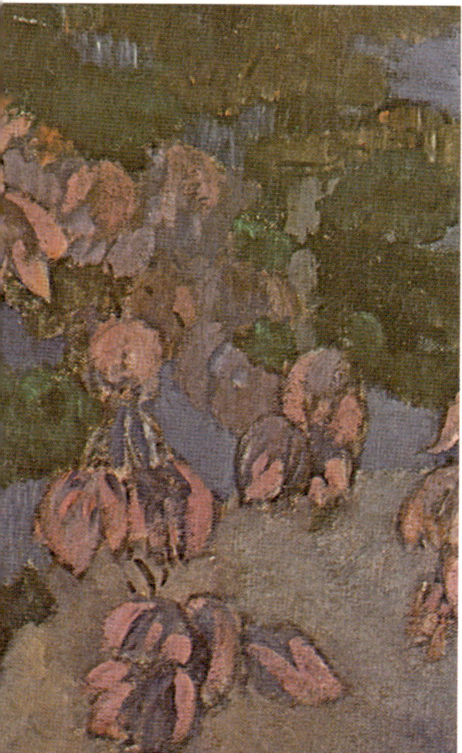

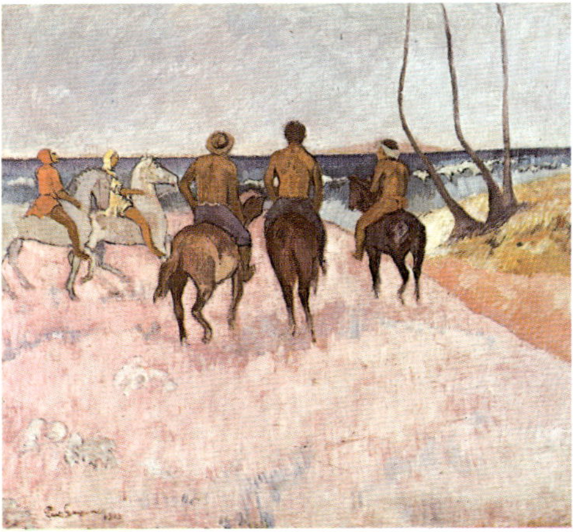

'Cavaliers sur la plage' (Horsemen on the beach) and detail (opposite), 1902.
Oil on canvas, 66 × 76 cm (26 × 30 in).
Essen, Folkwang Museum.

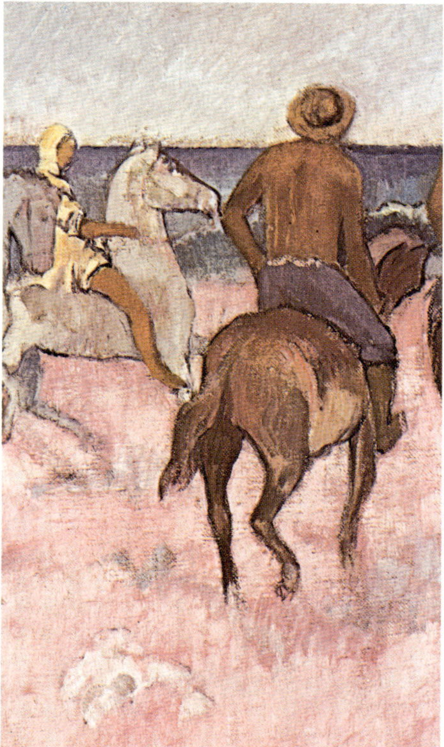

Title Index of Paintings